The Devil Wants YOU Busy, Bound and Burnt Out

Discover how you can stay on fire for
God and never experience burnout!

Barbara A. Desormo

WestBow
Press
A DIVISION OF THOMAS NELSON

Scripture taken from the King James Version of the Bible unless otherwise noted.

WestBow Press books may be ordered through booksellers or by contacting:

WestBow Press
A Division of Thomas Nelson
1663 Liberty Drive
Bloomington, IN 47403
www.westbowpress.com
1-(866) 928-1240

ISBN: 978-1-4497-6371-8 (sc)
ISBN: 978-1-4497-6373-2 (hc)
ISBN: 978-1-4497-6372-5 (e)

Library of Congress Control Number: 2012914807

Printed in the United States of America

WestBow Press rev. date: 11/07/2012

Contents

A Note Of Thanksgiving

First, I want to thank the Lord Jesus Christ for waking me up another day and giving me a life worth living. He has proven over and over again to be faithful—even when I'm not—and has been there for me in good times and bad times. I thank the Lord for every song and insight he has ever given me in my darkest hours. I value each and every one of them.

I thank God for my loving church family, who has been there for me at the First Baptist Church in Watertown, New York with Pastor Jeffrey Smith. I also want to say thank you to all those who have encouraged me and have helped me to overcome my fears to publish this book. You know who you are.

I thank God for Kim Kampnich along with Donna Bionidello and Denise Ivan from the Rose of Sharon Ministries. You are always there for me to pray, cry, and laugh with me and not at me. Thank you for allowing me to be me and use the gifts God has given me. You have been there as my spiritual cheerleaders to know who I am in Christ Jesus and to believe in myself and that I can do all things through Christ. Thank you, ladies at the Rose of Sharon. I am very thankful to be a part of this ministry.

This may sound strange, but I truly thank God for all who were not there in my life when I thought I needed them the most, because through it all, I had to trust in God to see me through every hardship. I have learned that just as David encouraged himself in the Lord, his God, it is possible to keep on keepin' on as long as my eyes are fixed on God, who is the author and finisher of my faith.

Introduction

Have you ever assumed that God would be pleased with every spiritual activity that you ever did? I know I have. After reading Matthew 7, I can picture many saying, "Lord, look at all the wonderful things I did for *you!* I prophesied in *your* name. I cast out devils in *your* name. I sang in the choir. I worked in the nursery at least three times a month, and I even gave beyond my tithes when the offering was taken—and I did it just for *you!*" I firmly believe that Jesus will tell many to depart from him, because they were too busy to take the time to really know him and what was really required of them. The Lord may even choose to pop a bubble or two by saying, "Are you braggin' or complainin'?" Or better yet, he may even say the very thing I have thought of saying when listening to people carry on about what they do: "*Who* told you that you had to?" I think people who brag either wanted to or they felt they had to do the things they did.

Please don't misunderstand me; works are good, and God expects us all to work. But for many, works has only served as dirt that many people use to bury all of their emotional pain and baggage. Many of us know that an idle mind is the Devil's workshop, but staying too busy can be just as detrimental when it comes to relationships. Therefore, *we must have balance!*

Genesis 4 says that Cain *worked* the soil, and in the course of time, he brought some of the fruits of that soil as an offering. Like us, Cain probably assumed God would be very pleased. After all, he worked very hard, so why wouldn't God be pleased? However, if you continue reading, you will see that God did not accept his offering. As a result, Cain was very angry. He then killed his brother, Abel. Cain was not only angry with his brother but also with God, because God did not accept his labor of love. Do you really believe that God accepts everything that we do for him if it is not done in faith, obedience, or with the right motive? How will you respond when God does not accept your offering or your labor of love? Will you respond as Cain did—in jealous anger or even murder?

Many times, we think we are doing many wonderful works in God's name. We truly believe that somehow, his name will be glorified if we keep on laboring. However, if God were to put the Holy Ghost's searchlight on our hearts and our work, we would find that we may be doing many wonderful things for all the wrong yet not-so-wonderful reasons. God is looking for those who love him and will obey him, because obedience is better than all of our sacrificial giving and works put together. If we love him, we will keep his commandments and obey him even if it means saying *no* to those who call us to go beyond the call of duty. You may even have to tell yourself *no!*

If you are a person who feels like they have to keep working I suggest you read this book. If you haven't taken time to enjoy life's journey with your Creator, then you need to find out why. There comes a time in our lives when we will need to prioritize our busy schedules. I pray that this book will do just that—help you to prioritize. The Devil wants you busy and bound, and he definitely wants you to be burnt out. He does *not* want you to enjoy your life or your relationships with God and others.

This book is divided into three sections. The first section deals with the many reasons that people go beyond the call of duty and *choose* to stay busy. Yes, believe it or not, some of us make that choice. You may not know all the reasons yet, but I believe you will know some by the time you finish this book. Some of the things that will be mentioned may serve as a springboard to discover other buried issues in your life as well.

The second section deals with the many reasons the Devil wants to keep us busy. In the final section are some answers that God has shared with me on how to overcome busyness and do only the Father's business.

After each chapter is a "Time to Reflect" section that will ask some soul- searching questions. You need to answer them as honestly as possible. Doing so could help you to find root problems as to why you personally go beyond the call of duty and take on more responsibilities than God—and even you—intended to take on.

I pray that you will not only take time out of your busy schedule to read this, but also earnestly open up your heart and let Jehovah Rophe (the healer) make you whole and free. You need to be free to enjoy life to the fullest. John 10:10 lets us know that there is a thief that comes to steal, kill, and destroy. He wants to destroy and kill your joy, peace, health, family, relationships, and even your life.

Titus 2:11 God's grace <u>has taught me</u> to say no and to start living a self-controlled life. Self-control does not only deal with our eating habits, how we spend our money, or how we use our tongues, but also lets me know that we need to be self-controlled in every area of our lives, including ministries, good deeds, and church activities. It is okay to say no! God's Word also teaches us that we are God's workmanship and that we were created to do good works. We can take on more than one activity and more than one ministry. However, when it comes to doing good works, it is better to do one thing well than to do more than one thing and be unfruitful or ineffective.

Read this very carefully: *if the Devil can't get you to quit, he will keep you busy!*

chapter 1

The Devil Just About Has A Hernia When We Learn To Say No!

Let's look at the lives of Moses and Pharaoh. God used Moses to go before the Pharaoh. Moses asked that Pharaoh let the children of Israel go. Pharaoh did not give up easily. He did not let the children of Israel go quickly for the same reasons we can't or won't let go quickly. His heart was hardened.

Whenever we refuse to let go of anything God requires of us, this unwillingness is an indication that we have a severe heart problem. (Yes, this is even true in the area of letting go of ministries and activities that produce no fruit.) Why wouldn't Pharaoh let the Israelites go? Why did he hang on so tightly? Why did it take so many plagues for him to finally say, "Okay, get outta town" and let the children of Israel go? I think we need to ask ourselves the same question. How long does it take you and me to let go and surrender our all to God? Not only is my heart hard, but I also must have a hard head as well. In spite of all the hard knocks along the road of life, I just don't seem to get it at times.

Before Pharaoh let the children of Israel go free, God sent many plagues his way to get his undivided attention. Some of them were the plague of frogs, flies, lice, hail, and finally, death. You can trust me when I say that God knows exactly how to get our attention.

I believe many of us have been plagued with one thing or another as well, because God is desperately trying to get our attention. God wants us to let go of the things in our lives that cause us to be too busy, bound, and eventually burnt out. There are some indicators that might help you realize if you are being plagued due to overload. First, let's talk about the plague of frogs.

In the account in Exodus 8, frogs were everywhere people looked. The people did not have to go very far to find the frogs. Everywhere they stepped, they probably stepped on a disgusting frog. Can you picture it—better yet, can you smell the odor? Many of us experience this plague, because everywhere we go, *we see something that needs to be done.* We think we have to jump in hook, line, and sinker to get the job done. We so want to be rid of the frogs or the workload, but we find ourselves saying the same thing as Pharaoh: "Tomorrow. Just let me get this done today, and tomorrow, I will slow down. I promise!" The truth is that yesterday is definitely gone, and there are no guarantees of tomorrow—but today is the day of new beginnings and salvation. Today is the day we must make new choices as to who and what we will serve.

We may not even know we are in the midst of burnout, but others will definitely know. Instead of hearing songs of praise coming from our mouths, all anyone will hear is croaking and complaining about all we do. If we are not careful and refuse to slow down, we just might croak someday from a heart attack or stroke. Believe it or not, the job will get done—even without us! I use the words *we* and *us,* because I am also guilty of not slowing down.

The second plague to examine is the plague of flies. Flies are annoying, and they love to swarm around us. You probably have heard those nagging sounds yourself. You know—*bzzzz!* Yes, you do know, because you have made that sound yourself. Listen to yourself: "I've been so *buzzzzy!*" "Honey,

2

I wish I could spend more time with you today—but maybe tomorrow, because today I am just too *buzzzzzzy.*" "Sorry, Lord, I don't have any time to read your Word or talk to you today. I have a *buzzzy* schedule today. I know you will understand." "I might be able to go and have lunch with you tomorrow, but the way my calendar looks, it appears that it is going to be another *buzzzy* day." I do not know which sounds the worst—the croaking of the frogs or the buzzing of those irritating flies.

Just as bees go from one hive to another to start new colonies, people with this plague go from one activity to the next, always starting new things, sometimes even before finishing the ones they have already started. (I am so busted!)

We know that whenever we see a vulture, it is a good indication that there is a carcass lying dead somewhere. When you see the carcass, you will probably see flies swarming around it as well. Sometimes we can walk into someone's home and find fruit flies swarming around a bowl of fruit. Even though most of the fruit displayed looks beautiful, if there are fruit flies, there has to be at least one piece of rotten fruit. God wants us to bear fruit, and he wants our fruit to remain. However, because of our busy schedules, the fruit of the Holy Spirit is beginning to decay, and others are able to see the tiny, disgusting fruit flies swarming around our rotten and probably stinking fruit. Many have the "stinkin' thinkin'" belief that they have to keep working around the clock.

Next is the plague of lice. Other than the fact that they are itchy, nasty, and contagious, there is one important factor worth mentioning—lice are tiny parasites that suck blood from people to stay alive. Lice and their eggs are very hard to see, but when the hair is pulled back or lifted from the neck and from behind the ears, you begin to see where these critters have sucked the very life out of someone.

Sometimes being too busy works the same way. Some of us feel life has been literally sucked out of us, because we do not know how to stop working. You feel drained, but you do not know why. You have to search your heart to find where the problem lies. More than likely, you are too busy and never found the rest that comes from sitting and listening at the feet of Jesus.

Fourth is the plague of hail. I have not experienced much hail in my life, but I do know that when hail falls, it is cold and hard. Hail, if out of control, can do a lot of damage to crops and other things. When we do not practice a life of self-control and life gets out of balance, especially in the area of how busy we are, we could find ourselves waxing cold very quickly. We find ourselves spending more and more time working and less time in the Word, prayer, and relationships. Relationships with God and others can be destroyed.

If you do not practice self-control, there will come a time when you will dread having to get up and get ready to go to the house of God. Just the thought of having to get up and go anywhere will become a chore. You will become hardened and cold to the things of God and to each other. This is definitely not a good place to be. There is nothing any colder than ashes after the fire has gone out! We need to stoke the cold ashes until the flames are burning brightly again in our lives. Just as cold hail can do much damage in the natural world, a lack of balance can do the same in the spiritual world. We need to guard our hearts with diligence to be certain this does not happen to us.

The last plague is the plague of death. First of all, there is spiritual death that separates us from God. This happens when we are too busy to spend the time with him that he desires and we desperately need. Second, there is the death of relationships with each other. Many marriages have ended in divorce because a spouse was married to his or her job. Putting in eight hours just wasn't enough. Work was taken home, and families were ignored. Do people and relationships have to die to get our attention? Not only is there death in our relationship with God and each other, but some people also literally work themselves to the grave.

Let's take time to read Exodus 5 and see what truths we can glean concerning Moses, Aaron, and the Pharaoh. First, however, you must understand that there is nothing wrong with working or doing good works. God expects *all* people to work. We also need to understand that regardless of how many good works you do, they will not buy or earn your salvation. We will not find special favor with God because of our good works, but we do good works because we have already found favor with God.

If you read Exodus 5:4–5, you will see how the Pharaoh asked both Moses and Aaron why they were taking the children of Israel away from their labor. Taking the Israelites away from their labor made the Pharaoh angry. He was so angry that he was almost to the point of having a hernia. He gave the taskmasters and officers orders not to give the children of Israel any more straw for making bricks. Even though straw was not provided, they were to still meet their quota in making just as many bricks as when the straw was provided.

You may ask what the big deal is. You have to understand that the Devil is a taskmaster. He is brutal, just like the Pharaoh, and he will keep demanding you to do more and more. The officers of the children of Israel were beaten, and the Egyptians demanded to know why the Israelites had not fulfilled their task in making as many bricks as when straw was provided for them. The Enemy will always keep you feeling like you have never met and will never meet your quota or share of the workload.

Romans 8:1 tell us that there is now no condemnation to those who are in Christ Jesus—who walk not after the flesh but walk after the Spirit. We must be led of the Holy Spirit and walk after the Spirit in what God wants or does not want us to do; otherwise we will beat ourselves up in condemnation and feel that we can never meet our quota or do enough. Moses was to go before the Pharaoh to let the people of Israel go so the Israelites could go a three-day journey into the desert and sacrifice to the Lord, their God. The Devil will do everything he can to keep you and I busy to keep us from offering true worship to the true and living God. He is deceitful. If not careful, you and I will fall for his trap every time. Just as Pharaoh wanted the Israelites bound as slaves, the Devil wants us bound up. His job is to find ways to keep you and me working from sun up to sundown. He does not want you to enjoy your life.

The Devil wants everything but for you to enjoy anything. He wants you tired, on the edge, and burnt out. If Christians are truly functioning under God's grace and are led by the Holy Spirit, then why are they are so tired and disgruntled? Why do they keep on complaining about how much they have done, are doing, and have not yet accomplished? There are many people who are addicted to work—even to the point of burnout—yet they keep on volunteering their time and efforts. That is not God's plan!

I listen to people more attentively these days. I listen to them as they talk to me about what they *have to do* for the Lord. I emphasize the words *have to do*, because their tasks sound more like the duties of a slave than those of a servant. I desperately want to remind them that the Word says that while serving the Lord, we need to serve him with gladness. Instead of gladness, I hear dread, despair, and even depression at times, but no joy. I would dare say that I even hear the sound of death in my ears. This is not God's plan for anyone's life.

If you do not have time to fellowship with the Lord in daily Bible reading and prayer, then you might consider the fact that you are busy! If you do not have time to build a relationship with God, your family, and God's family, then you are too busy! You are either busy doing what you want to do, what you think you must do, or what others expect of you. It is time that we, the church, set our priorities straight if we are going to be effective in the kingdom. We need to seek God and find out exactly what he expects of us. We need to *stop doing* what others want us to do—or even what we want to do. I know it is not going to be easy, but with God's help, we can and will get our priorities straight. I believe that if we seek God first, we will get everything done that he wants. If we let *him* complete the work that he began in us, then he can and will complete his work through us.

The Pharaoh made sure that straw was not provided for the Israelites to get the job done. However, God has provided everything we need to get done what He wants to get done. He will provide the time, finances, etc. so we can do what he wants to do through us if we will but let Him!

Prayer: Father, I come to you today as humbly as I know how. I ask you to show me what it is you want me to do. There are people in darkness who you want to reach through me. I am to be the light that shines in the darkness, but I admit to you I am burning my candle at both ends, and I am getting burnt out. Help me to get my priorities in line with your Word and your will for my life. I want to serve you with gladness in my heart. In Jesus name – Amen!

Are we serving the Lord with gladness, as servants,
or are we grudgingly working as slaves?

Time To Reflect

1. How many days a week do you read your Bible? How long do you read for?
2. How many days a week do you pray? How long do you pray?
3. How much time do you spend with your family?
4. How much time do you spend with God's family?
5. How much time do you spend at work?
6. How much time do you spend taking work home with you?
7. How much time do you spend doing church activities?
8. What is your mind preoccupied with during Bible reading or prayer?
9. What do you do for rest and relaxation?
10. When was the last time you took your family out for a fun day?
11. When was the last time you and your spouse had a real date?
12. When was the last time you played a game with your kids?

If it's been a while since you had a date with your spouse or spent quality time doing fun things with the family, then you might consider the fact that you are too busy! You need to find time to do important things, such as building relationships.

Just as seven days make one week, seven days of all
work and no play will make one weak!

chapter 2

Assurance Of Salvation

As I read the Psalms one morning, I felt the Lord prompt me to turn to the book of Mark. I never thought God worked that way. "What do you mean, Lord? You are asking me to turn to the book of Mark when I am reading the Psalms?" Religion says we have to read according to the daily schedule to read the Bible in a year. "The Psalms bring me comfort, and I sure could use some comforting words these days."

At first, I did not know where to begin. I started to read Mark 10 about the rich young ruler. I really believe that God knew where I would begin to read when he told me to turn there. In the 17th verse, the rich young ruler called Jesus 'good' and then proceeded to ask Jesus what he *must do* to inherit eternal life. Wow! Did you read that like I read that? *Right from* the very beginning, before people even received eternal life through Christ, they thought salvation was all about what they have to do instead of what Christ has already done.

The young ruler asked what he had to do in order to inherit eternal life. Come to think of it, I can't recall anyone having to do a thing to inherit anything. In order for anyone to inherit anything, someone else did all the work and then left a beneficiary when they died (no disrespect intended). All we have to do is *receive our inheritance by faith.* Someone else pays the price, and someone else dies. Isn't that a perfect picture of what Christ did for us? He paid the highest price for us with his own blood when He died at Calvary.

The jail keeper in Acts 16 asked Paul, "What *must I do* to be saved?" Many people, including myself, always seem to think salvation has to do with working and doing. In God's dictionary, *religion* is spelled "D-O-I-N-G," and *relationship* is spelled "D-O-N-E." There was nothing this young rich ruler or jail keeper in Acts 16 did or could ever do that would save them. There is nothing that we have done, are doing, or ever will do that can save us either. Nothing can be added to our salvation. Christ has done it *all* already at Calvary. It is finished. All we have to do is receive it by faith. We are saved by grace through faith in Christ Jesus. He even went on to say, "Not by works!"{Ephesians 2:8}It is not the works of baptism, church attendance, or 1,001 active yet ineffective ministries. We are saved by grace. Did you get that? We cannot earn salvation or work for our salvation.

However, because of salvation, we will want to do good works. When one truly receives Christ, I believe he or she will want to get involved in the local church—but I also believe that there has to be balance. That is what this book is all about—*motives and balance!* We should be doing only the things that God asks us to do. I do know that many will disagree with me, but I find the ones I know who disagree with me are frazzled to no end. We must let God place us where he wants us to be.

Just as the rich young ruler and the jail keeper thought they had to do something before salvation, this pattern continues even after salvation. Many of us feel the need to keep doing—but we keep doing for all the wrong reasons. I want you to find out why you think you have to keep on working and doing when God wants you to have life and freedom. He wants every last one of his children to enjoy their lives, themselves, and others as they serve him to the fullest.

Some Christians—even great Christian leaders—have a tendency to judge those who do not get involved in a lot of different ministries like they do. Could it be that the reason some do not get involved is because God has not asked them to help in the area they are being asked to help out in? Don't get me wrong; I believe God wants us all to get involved in his work. However, if *you* are doing the calling, don't expect others to be anointed to do whatever it is that you are calling them to do. This does not mean that they can't be helpers or try to see where they belong. I am *only* talking to people who are out of balance and just don't know how to say no. They might be accused of being lazy or not having a concern or burden; even Pharaoh accused the children of Israel of being idle or slothful.

I have known many Christians who have complained to me or have quit church because people put them to work doing something that they did not feel called or led to do. They ended up frustrated and quit. I compare working in the wrong ministry to trying to walk in a size three shoe when you should be wearing a size ten. A ministry may not seem to fit for someone you ask to do certain tasks. That area is not only uncomfortable, but also hurts as others try to fit into something that God has not custom fit for their lives.

A lady recently told me why she committed to doing something in her home absolutely free of charge. I was totally shocked when she told me why she took on the responsibility—because that way she could tell people at church she could not take on any more responsibilities at church. I did not know whether to laugh or cry. Why can't we just say no to people? Here is a better question—why is it that we cannot say no to people but we can say no to God? We do it all the time. When we do not do what he wants us to do and keep doing the things he has not asked us to do, we are saying yes to people and no to God. This is something to really think about! We will fall into the category of being people-pleasers.

We can have blessed assurance of our salvation not because of what we have done but because of what Christ has already done at Calvary. It is finished! Quit adding to his great plan of redemption!

Prayer: Father, I thank you that I am saved by your grace. Continually teach me to understand that I can't work for it, earn it, or buy it but that it is a free gift. All I have to do is to receive it by faith. In Jesus name – Amen!

Time To Reflect

1. Have you received Christ as your personal Savior?
2. What did you have to *do* to receive salvation?
3. What has Christ *done* for you to obtain salvation?
4. How do you know you are saved?
5. What is God calling or asking you to do?
6. Are you doing anything that God has not asked you to do? Why or why not?
7. How do you feel when you *know* you are doing what God has called you to do? Do you feel at peace? Do you have joy?
8. How do you feel when you do things God has not called you to do?
9. Do you have *religion,* or do you have a *relationship* with Christ?

I am not saying you have to say no if someone asks you to do something, but I am asking you to pray first. I am speaking to people who for one reason or another just cannot say *no!*

You need to get a life! Do you want God's abundant life?
Slow down!

chapter 3

What Are You Caught Up In?

I need to begin with a song that the Lord gave me many years ago. The song inspired this book. It's not a long song, and it doesn't even have a fancy tune or a very popular beat. Nevertheless, the lyrics are very powerful. Examine your heart as you read the words.

Why do you do the things you do? Lyrics and music by Barb Desormo

Why do you do the things you do
Is a question that I'm asking you?
Do you do it to please the Master?
Or is your hand reaching out
For the praise of men
Time and again
If you are, then your motives are wrong.
So listen very carefully to my little song.
Who do you love?
The creature or Creator
Which do you love—?

The giver or the gift
Which do you love—?
The praise of men or Jesus
Three out of six,
Take your pick
On whom and which do you love

Many of us are caught up in a trap of "doing" for many reasons. We have an internal drive. We feel like our world will come to an end if we can't do something. Is this you? Personally, I cannot even stand to drive using cruise control, because I feel I should be doing something, not the cruise control. There are at least three reasons listed in the song above for doing the things we do.

Do we love the gift or do we love the giver of the gift? There are many who think they are in love with the giver of the gift, but in all truth, they really love the gift or gifts. For some reason, gifts just seem to make us feel more spiritual. The more gifts and talents we have the more spiritual we tend to feel. It is almost as if our works, talents, and gifts serve as a barometer of our spirituality. Do we love the praise of men, or do we wait to hear, "Well done, thou good and faithful servant" from God?

How do you feel when no one seems to see what you have done? How do you feel when others are recognized and you are not? How do you feel when you can do and say the same things others do and say and go unnoticed while they receive recognition? To be perfectly honest with you, when others are recognized for the things I did or said, I get somewhat annoyed, and my feathers are ruffled.

God did not intend us to be doing things twenty-four hours a day, seven days a week. Even God knew he needed to take a day and rest. After all, He had to rest on the seventh day, because he made man on the sixth. {That's one of my original jokes} God knew that his work was cut out for him when he created us humans. Jesus, as a man, got tired and had to have some down time somewhere all by himself to pray. If God had to rest on the seventh day so he could look back and enjoy his creation, and if Jesus had to stop working and get away from the multitudes, shouldn't we follow the same example?

He told us to keep the Sabbath holy—a commandment all of us need to consider. I believe if we all did this, we would all be healthier, have more energy, and would live longer, more fulfilled lives. Find a day and time each week that you can call your Sabbath, and then cease from all your labors.

John 10:10 states that there is a thief who comes to steal, kill, and destroy. The Enemy will do his best to rob from your life. He loves to destroy families and relationships in the name of *work*. However, Jesus came that we might have life and life more abundantly. We all need to put on our combat boots, go into the Enemy's territory, and take back what rightfully belongs to us. I don't know about you, but I want all God has for my life. I want energy to enjoy my husband, children, and grandchildren and my great grandson. That can and will happen if I choose to do only the things God requires of me.

Matthew 7:21 said it all so well. He said that not everyone who says, "Lord, Lord" will enter the kingdom. They will remind God of all that they have done for him and how they did it in his name. I can hear us now; can you? "Lord, don't you remember all the wonderful works that I did?"

What was God's response? He flat-out said, "To depart from me," because he never knew them. They were so caught up in themselves and their many wonderful works that they were unable to have any kind of relationship with him—or anyone else, for that matter. Jesus told them to depart from him, because he never knew them. I did not say it—God did.

When we do something for the Lord, do we toot our horns? I only know of one horn that we should be concerned about. It will not toot; it will be the sound of a trumpet blast, And the dead in Christ shall rise first. Then those who are alive and remaining will be caught up to be with Jesus forevermore. Will you be ready?

Jesus is coming back soon to catch His bride away. Don't be so caught up in all your wonderful works that you miss him!

Time To Reflect

1. Do you find it hard to say *no*? If so, then why?
2. Do you feel driven to work?
3. Do you find it hard to just sit down and be still? Read Psalm 23.
4. What happens during your quiet time with the Lord? Is your mind working overtime with things you have to do?
5. Can you stay at a task for any given amount of time, or do you think about all the things that you have to *do*?
6. Are you able to keep one day a week holy as a Sabbath, doing absolutely nothing?
7. Has the Devil stolen your joy? Your peace? Your family? What are you going to do about it?
8. Reread the lyrics of the song and answer all the questions that are listed in the song.

The style of popular music has changed over the years, but the message of the gospel—the good news—has not changed. The bad news is that if you don't take time to smell the roses, then you will never discover what the good news has to say about your future.

Prayer: Father, I admit that I feel driven to keep doing even when you Want me to cease from all *my* labor and just rest in you. I ask you to search my heart and show me why I do the things that I do. Do I love you as my Creator? Do I love the gifts you gave me more than you—the giver of all gifts? Do I love to hear the praises of men, or do I desire to hear, "Well done, thou good and faithful servant; enter into the joy of the Lord"? Lord, I know that one day your children will be caught up in the air to meet you. Please help me not to be so caught up in my own plans, agendas, and works that I miss it. Help me to keep the Sabbath holy unto you. In Jesus name – Amen!

God's plans are to prosper you, not to harm you. His plans are to give you a hope and a future. Your plans to prosper and have a future could kill you!

chapter 4

Acceptance

Ephesians 2 specifically Tells workaholics that they are saved through faith. Grace is a free gift. As I said earlier, we cannot work or labor for it. We cannot buy our salvation, because God has already purchased it for us at Calvary. He paid the highest price when he shed his blood at Calvary's cross to purchase us!

Let's look in Genesis chapters 29 and 30 at the lives of two very important women who were in Jacob's life. There are many truths from the lives of Leah and Rachel that we can glean, but first let me give you a little background as to what happened. Jacob worked seven years for Rachel. Because of his love for her, the Word says, those seven years seemed like only a few days. Unfortunately, after the seven years were up, Jacob was not given the woman of his dreams. He woke up and found himself with Rachel's older sister, Leah. There's a shocker for you. How many of us married our spouses, thinking we knew who they were, only to find *after* we married them that they were not the people we thought they were? Don't laugh, because your spouse got a little surprise as well.

Jacob eventually received Rachel, but he had to work seven more years. Don't think for a moment that Leah was not aware that Jacob loved Rachel and that he would go to great lengths to be in a relationship with her. In case you did not know it, God has also gone to great lengths to be in a loving relationship with us by sending his Son to die for us and giving us his Holy Spirit.

When the Lord saw that Leah was hated, he opened her womb. Most women that I know want their husbands to love them. This was the case with Leah. She desperately wanted Jacob, her husband, to love her. As a result, she labored. She did not work, but she labored having children, hoping that someday, Jacob would love and accept her as well. As I meditated on this particular portion of Scripture, God revealed to me that Leah could be a type of person who thinks she can obtain God's favor by laboring (finding favor by our works).

I want you to pay particular attention to how Leah named all of her sons. Leah made a very strong and profound statement after each of her children was born. She named her first son Reuben, meaning, the LORD has looked upon my affliction. After all, the Lord saw her misery and how much she suffered. She said, "Now my husband will love me." How many have felt that the more they suffer, the more God will love and accept them? That kind of thinking is sad, because some think they suffer for the sake of righteousness, but in all reality, they suffer because of their choices or because they take on too many responsibilities.

Marriages, friendships, relationships between children and parents, and health issues are only a few things that suffer when people take on too many responsibilities that God never intended. Some feel that if they can obtain the favor of God, then all the suffering they go through will be worth it. They also feel their good works of church attendance, giving, feeding the poor, reading their Bibles, teaching Sunday school classes, etc. will cause God to love and accept them. These are all good works, but they don't and will never earn God's love and acceptance.

Grace is a free gift, and that is how we are saved. We are saved by grace through faith in Christ Jesus—nothing more. We are not saved by what we have done, are doing, or ever will do, but because of what Jesus did. When he said, "It is finished," nothing more could be added. We are to do good works because of salvation, but we do not do good works to receive salvation. However, because we are saved, our desire should be to do only God's will.

One may not desire to teach Sunday school. *Oh no—no desire to teach? Every born-again Christian should desire to teach a class, right?* A thousand times "No." A person may not have a desire to teach, because God may not call them to teach. He or she may be gifted to do something totally different. That person may have a desire to sing and even the ability to sing, but that does not mean that he or she is called to lead worship or the church choir. We all need to seek the Lord to find our place in the body of Christ. God places every member where it pleases him.

Doing one or many works does not guarantee us salvation. Just as works will not guarantee us salvation, we must understand that salvation is not a sure guarantee that we will be called to be pastors (or any other work we may desire). Let me explain! You may have a desire to be a pastor or a missionary. These are great desires, but salvation will not guarantee us that God will call us to be such.

I have learned this the hard way. Even when I did many good works, the fact remained that God did not call me to do many of the things I did. So why did I stay so busy? I did many good works, because I still had not learned of God's grace. I always felt I had to earn God's favor by doing good works. I felt the more I worked, the more God loved me. I kept working and proclaiming that I labored *in love* when in all reality, I was actually laboring *for God's love*, just as Leah labored for Jacob's love when she labored to give him children. There is a difference! Leah wanted to please Jacob; she hoped he would love her in return. She named the rest of her sons for the following reasons. She gave birth to Simeon and said, "Because the LORD hath heard that I was hated" in Genesis 29:33. She had a son, Levi, and then said, "Now this time my husband will be joined unto me, because I have born him three sons [Genesis 29:34]. Do you see or hear the turmoil that went on in this poor woman's life?

Many of us are no different. When you fall into this trap, you will find yourself entangled and in this same bondage. You will keep laboring, as Leah did, and then wonder later what happened. After a mother gives birth to so many kids, she feels she has nothing left to offer anyone. She has no energy to do anything. She has divided herself up in so many directions that she no longer feels like a whole woman. It is no different in the spiritual realm.

That is one reason the Devil wants you busy. He wants you to be good for nothing. He does not want you to feel like a whole person. He wants you to be in a place where you have nothing to offer anyone—including yourself.

Now let's bring Rachel on the scene. She was loved by Jacob. Jacob worked another seven years, knowing there was a possibility that Uncle Laban, Rachel and Leah's father, might trick him again. Nevertheless, he took his chances. Nothing Rachel did would make Jacob love her any less or more than he already did. However, this was not enough for Rachel. She was not content with the love that Jacob had for her. She felt a strong need to have children, or she felt she would die. It was a disgrace for a woman in Bible times not to bear children; however, I believe there were many more unresolved issues in Rachel's heart.

Leah and Rachel were sisters! Genesis 30 tells us that when Rachel saw that she was not giving children to Jacob, she became jealous of Leah. When Naphtali was born, Leah had the guts to say, "I have had a great struggle with my sister, and I have won." In case you haven't noticed, there was a battle going on. The sisters competed against each other. There was and is a competitive spirit dwelling in the land, and it has crept into the church. Ephesians 6 tells us that we are in no way fighting against flesh and blood. When we do not accept the love that God has for us, we do the same thing these two sisters did. We begin to compare ourselves with others. That competitive spirit takes root and slowly begins to control us if we are not careful. We don't have to compare or compete when we know we are loved and accepted by our Bridegroom. We can have complete peace with him, others, and ourselves. Ephesians 1:6 is one of my favorite passages. We are all the accepted of the beloved if we have received him as our personal Savior.

Genesis 30:22 records that God remembered Rachel; he listened to her and opened her womb. Finally, Rachel got her miracle. Rachel gave birth to a son. Even though God gave her the desire of her heart and gave her a son, Rachel still struggled. How do I know this? You can tell much about a person by a name—their own or a name she gives to her children. Rachel named her son Joseph. You may think, *"What is the big deal?"* *Hey, Joseph is a great name.* After all, it is a name we all can pronounce; most Bible names are difficult to do so. Joseph was a man of character, prestige, and power! However, Rachel naming her son Joseph reveals to me that there were more unresolved issues in her life. Rachel was still competing with her sister, Leah. The love Jacob had for Rachel still was not enough for her.

Rachel was not content with Jacob's love or with the fact that God opened her womb and gave her the desire of her heart by giving her a son. Because she was not content, she was still competing with her sister.

I mentioned earlier that when Jesus said, "It is finished," nothing more could be added? Joseph's name reveals more heart issues with Rachel. Rachel named her son and said, "Add to me another son." His name means "to add" or "adding." When would Rachel get it? Rachel did not have to compete with her sister for Jacob's love, but she did. Until you know the love that the Father has for you, you will always compare and compete with others. This revelation has freed me. Jacob loved Rachel just the way she was. What more can a woman want or need? She should have left it at that! However, Rachel, in her discontentment, wanted Jacob to give her another son.

God gave Rachel the desire of her heart again. We all need to be careful what we ask for! The children of Israel were given manna daily, and they were also discontented. Discontentment leads to murmuring, and murmuring can lead to death. In Numbers 11:31-34 the children of Israel cried for meat, and God gave them meat, just as they desired. However, the end result was nothing to be desired. God never gave them a chance to grab a toothpick and pick the meat from their teeth. They died with the meat between their teeth.

Unfortunately for Rachel, bad news came with her little bundle of joy. God gave Rachel exactly what she wanted. God gave her another son, just as she desired; however, this time, Rachel died giving birth to Benjamin. Rachel got what she wanted—but what about Benjamin? Benjamin did not have a mother. Do you really think he wanted to live with the fact that his mother died giving birth to him? She wanted to name him Ben-oni (son of my sorrow), but Jacob said he would be called Benjamin (son of my right hand).

Sometimes God loves us so much that he will give us the desires of our heart and then whip us with it. You need to understand this not only in your head, but also in your heart and spirit. Just as Rachel died giving birth to Benjamin because she wanted God to add to her another son, adding to the word and to our salvation can also result in spiritual death! Salvation by God's grace is a free gift of life and peace. Why do we continually think we have to add anything? God gives us everything we need; yet we are always discontented. We want God to add another ministry, job, child, spouse, or credit card. *Discontentment is death! Don't ask God to keep adding.* As Leah and Rachel kept competing with each other, there was division between the two sisters.

God showed me a very profound truth when using math. We must remember when doing a math problem that involves division, there is always subtraction involved when trying to solve the problem. Whenever there is division caused by disagreements in a church among brothers or sisters, there will also not only be division, but also subtraction. God adds to the church those who should be saved; however, we need to add to our faith, as stated in 2 Peter 1:5-7.

Jacob loved Rachel. He paid the price for her. We are God's chosen people. He purchased us; he paid the price for us. We do not have to labor, work, and beg for his acceptance or love. When we know that his love is complete in us, we no longer have to compare ourselves or compete with others. We will have confidence on the Day of Judgment when we know his love is complete in us. Many who think salvation has to be earned or feel they have to labor will stand before God. I wonder how many will remind him of the many times they have prophesied in his name or how many devils they casted out. Will they stand before him and tell him how many wonderful works they did in his name? Some might! However, what child has to remind his parents what he has done for them? What parent should have to remind his child of all that he has done for that child? If he does, the relationship is probably not very stable.

Unfortunately, God will tell these people to depart from him, because he never knew them. It does not matter how many works we have done, as wonderful as they may seem. It's not about how many titles we possess, positions we fill, or ministries we can keep adding to what we already have.

If you do not have a personal relationship with God, your works mean nothing. Without love, our good deeds profit us nothing!

Now let's look at the life of Joseph (Rachel's son). Joseph knew that he was loved and accepted by his father, Jacob. His father loved him so much that he gave Joseph a coat of many colors {Genesis 37}. There came a time that Joseph's brothers stripped him of his coat, and Jacob thought he was dead. Joseph might have lost his coat of many colors, but God revealed to me that the coat was only a token of his father's love. Joseph never lost sight of the fact that his father truly loved him. I believe the love that Jacob had toward Joseph sustained and encouraged Joseph in his deepest trials and in his darkest pit. There are many who could be set free from the pit of depression and despair if they just realized how much Father God loves them.

Many of us are in love with our gifts but not the giver of the gifts. Many of us also feel that the more gifts the Father bestows or gives to us, the more he loves us as well. We use the gifts as a barometer of how much he loves us. We also use people as a barometer—whether people show appreciation for our gifts. If many people show up to a class that we teach, then we feel we found God's favor. If they don't show up, then somehow we feel like failures and go into a deep pit of depression.

God had to teach me that numbers mean nothing to Him. In other words, Christ died for the one as well as the multitude. When we feel stripped of God's spiritual tokens, (anointing, call, gifts, talents, etc.), we somehow feel we can't go on in life. That is hogwash! You must first fall in love with the giver of the gifts. Joseph was a perfect example of Romans 8 when it said that *nothing or nobody* could separate him from the love of God, which is in Christ Jesus. Nothing or nobody could separate him from the love he had toward his father or the love his father had toward him. They were inseparable.

For some reason, Rachel could not grasp the love that Jacob had for her any more than I can grasp the love the Father has for me. However, you must realize that even though you love someone, you can still become angry with him or her. In Genesis 30: 2 Jacob became angry with Rachel when she said she would die if he did not give her children. He even asked her if he was in the place of God, who kept her from having children? Jacob knew he could not make things happen any more than we can. Rachel's ability to have children was totally out of his control when God closed her womb.

Remember, when God opens a door, no man can shut it, and when God closes a door, no man can open it. This was true of Rachel's ability to have children. It had to be from God, or nothing would happen. We must all come to the conclusion that if God is not in the things that we do, everything else may be good for nothing as well. This is a lesson we all should learn. Unless the Lord builds the house, we will all labor, but we will only labor in vain. The builder is God—not us. Everything is about God; not about me—and not about you, either.

Today, I watered my philodendron plant. Before I watered them, I had to take off many dead leaves. As I pulled the dead ones off, I thought about all the things that I do that choke the very life from me. I believe God wants us to pick or pluck the activities in our lives that do not produce fruit. My plant had come to a complete standstill. It looked sickly, and it stunk as I held the dead leaves in my hands. My granddaughter, Hanna, did not understand what I was doing. I explained to her that all of the dead leaves had stunted the growth of the plant.

Asking God to add more activities in your life will only make you a stinking and sickly Christian whose growth will be forever stunted. Please be content and accept the love the Father has for you. You can quit competing with your brothers and sisters in Christ. You are not in competition. Be content with the fact that God chose you because he loves you. You did not choose him; he chose and ordained you to go and bring forth fruit so that your fruit would remain. How can you bring forth fruit unless you first pluck off the activities that do not produce life?

I truly believe as Jacob became angry with Rachel because she expected him to give her only what God could give to her, I believe God can become angry with us when we are not contented with what he has given us. We all need to quit asking God to keep adding. We need gratitude for what we have and get rid of our attitude for what we don't have.

Prayer: Father God, please help me realize just how much you love and accept me for who I am. Even though you accept me for who I am, you love me too much to keep me this way. Help me when I start to compare myself with others or compete for the love that you have so freely given to me. I Don't want to be like Leah and feel that I have to labor for your love. I don't want to be discontented, ask you to keep adding, and then experience both spiritual and physical death. I want to know that you love me as Joseph knew his father loved him and sustained him through his deepest pit and darkest trial. Let nothing separate me from your love. In Jesus' name, amen!

Time To Reflect

1. How do you know God loves you?
2. Who do you think of when you think of the love Jacob had for Rachel?
3. Who does Leah remind you of?
4. How are the lives of Leah and Rachel similar to your life? How are they different?
5. How would you describe the relationship between Rachel and her sister, Leah?
6. Both Rachel and Leah competed against each other. Do you find yourself competing against anyone? If so, why?
7. Do you compare yourself with others? If so, why?
8. What do you think you have to do to receive acceptance from God or others?
9. What truth have you learned from this chapter?
10. How will you apply what you have learned from this chapter?

I have read the passage of Scripture in John 8:32 concerning truth many times. If we know the truth, then the truth will make us free. I always took this Scripture to mean that I must know the Word. After all, the Word is truth. However, it is not enough to know what truth is; you must also know who truth is. John 14 tells us that Jesus is not only the way and the life, but also the truth. Truth is a person, and when we get to know him and his Word, we will be made free.

The King James Version says we will be made free, but other translations mention that we will be set free. I believe that being made free is very different from being set free. To set something free is instantaneous; yet making something free is a process. It takes time. Spending time with God helps the process along. We will no longer have to compete or compare ourselves with anyone. All we will be concerned about is that God approves of us and accepts us if we are in obedience.

You can choose to either do things God's way and see your dreams fulfilled or do them your way and wake up to your greatest nightmare!

chapter 5

Assumptions

God shared something with me that was a real eye-opener. He gently reminded me that I never liked it when my children assumed anything, and he does not like it when his children assume things, either. *Ouch!* Why do we assume God will be pleased with all the wonderful works we do? I know there are times when I have asked my children to vacuum the floor or fold clothes. Instead, they assumed I would be pleased if they did something else, such as mopping the floors or washing clothes that had to be washed on the gentle cycle. If I told them to sweep or vacuum, that is what I meant. I knew for them to mop would be a disaster, so I did not want them to do that.

Scripture tells us in I Samuel 15:22 that to obey is better than sacrifice. I believe that sacrifice falls under the category of works. All of our works, regardless of how good they are, can and never will take the place of obedience. Some assume that God will tell them how wonderful they are as they do all their wonderful works, but he will not tell them such wonderful news. He will tell them to depart from him, because he never knew them. Just because people do many wonderful works, never assume that they know God. They can know about him but never know him. David had a great desire, and he assumed it would be okay to do something spiritual, but God said *no!* Now, if God can say no, don't you think it is all right for us to do the same?

In I Chronicles 28:1-5 both Nathan and David assumed that God would allow David to build the temple. David told Nathan the desire of his heart, and Nathan told him to go for it. This was not so! God gave Nathan a word concerning David's desire to build, and then Nathan had to tell David to put his desires on the back burner as far as building was concerned. God had something totally different in mind. David did absolutely none of the building; yet he played a very significant part in seeing the temple built in its entirety.

How would you have responded if you were David? Would you have been upset? If you are a workaholic, you could have been upset very easily. David did not respond in a negative way when he was told he could not build. David was able to acknowledge the fact that God called him to be a king; God called Judah as a leader; and God called David's son, Solomon, to build the temple. Unless you know where God has placed you in the body of Christ, you won't know how to say no, and you won't know how to take no for an answer. God will constantly say to you, "What part of *no* don't you understand?" It is best to know who God has called for the hour, where God has called you, accept the fact, and then move on!

When you realize and accept the fact that God has called your pastor to be the pastor and has called you to be the one to clean the toilets, you will be better off. People who desire to be leaders and are not called need to know right up front that their brother or sister is the leader and that they are called to do something else. Many people also *assume* that because they have a gift to sing or play an instrument, God is calling them to lead worship in their local church. God might be calling them to lead worship, but not in the sanctuary for all eyes to behold. God just might be calling them to lead worship with the toddlers or in children's church. He might be calling them to take their talents to the nursing homes or prisons. Sorry if this offends, but it is truth.

We assume because we are gifted or have certain talents, God called us to be the leader of the pack. However, I believe when you say yes to God when he calls you to ministries that others may not find desirable, you will have joy and peace that pass all human understanding. There is no greater satisfaction than being where God wants you. I have seen people in exalted positions who were truly miserable, and I have also seen people who do lowly tasks that no one else would want who are content, because they know God has planted them there, and they blossom.

For many of my Christian years, I was only asked to be a substitute as far as teaching. I hate to admit it, but I got a little ticked off, because I was not content being a substitute. I remember grumbling to God as I sorted the laundry. I bent over to pick some clothes off the floor, and I told God just how sick and tired I was of being a substitute. Before I was able to stand back up, God reminded me how his Son became my substitute and went to the cross in my place, because no one else would or could. That shut my complaining up very quickly. It humbled me as well. I never complained about where God placed me after that.

God has shared some insights with me that have changed my way of thinking and set me free. I hope they will help you also. You can read the account of David in 1 Chronicles 28–29. David desired to build a house for God, but instead, God had chosen David's son, Solomon, to build the temple. Fortunately, David knew how to take no for an answer. It would be easy to assume that David became discouraged and threw in the towel. If you think David just sat back and did nothing, guess again. David played a very significant part in the temple being built in its entirety without ever putting a tool belt around his waist or lifting a hammer to drive a nail. Like David, we can have a part in seeing God's kingdom being built in a very significant way. We must humble ourselves, accept where God places us, and do what he wants and not what others (or we) want.

David had a spiritual desire, and he planned to build a house for the Lord. However, it was not God's will at all, because David was a man of war. How many of us (including me) mistake a spiritual desire for the call of God? You can have all the desire you want, but there is a slight possibility God may not call you to build or start a certain ministry. He may, or he may not. You must then make a choice, accept that fact, and move on to where God wants you. This may not be easy. Second, you must diligently seek God, and ask God where he wants you. We all can have a great part in seeing God's purpose fulfilled if we just stay in tune with the Holy Spirit and do only what he wants us to do. When you really want to see God's purpose fulfilled, it just won't matter who does what as long as the job gets done. That is called maturity and true ministry!

It is vital that you realize that the Spirit gave David the blueprints on how to build the temple. Instead of David assuming he was to build, David willingly passed those plans on to Solomon once he knew it was God's will for him to do so. How many of us could pass a Spirit-led blueprint that God gave to us on to others? Many people have been gifted to think very creatively, but when it came time to actually put things together, they needed the help of others. I believe God gives me creative ideas, but I cannot see them through, because I have no artistic ability. Therefore, I do not find it difficult to release my ideas to someone else. However, if I had both creative thoughts and artistic abilities, I believe I would have a much harder time releasing my ideas.

Can you imagine being a great artist and then being told you have to pass your brush and palette filled with beautiful colors for someone else to paint for you? I cannot fathom that happening to me. Songwriters may experience the same situation. They write songs, but others may sing the songs God gave them. This is the situation David was in. He had the passion and creative plan given to him by the Spirit, but then he was put to the test. However, David not only passed the test, but also willingly passed those plans on to his son. The blueprint really belongs to God.

If God gave me the plans and the ability to see a project through, I truly believe I would struggle with releasing the plans to God's anointed one. I know I would feel that God was calling me to do it all. Whenever you pass on the blueprints, *you must release them completely!* How many times have we released a position to someone and yet held on at the same time? You must trust that Jesus will do the work. If God trusted you with the blueprints, then you need to trust the one both God and you entrusted the plans to. Did God tell you to trust that person with the plans? If God did not tell you to give the plans to someone, then you might have something to worry about. For some, passing work along is not easy to do—especially for a workaholic.

Come on, you need to delegate as far as the work that needs to be done and take your hands off. Let go, and let God!

David took silver and gold out of his treasury for the temple to be built with such splendor. What if you are given the blueprint of a project? Are you still willing to give out of your treasury to see the fruition of someone else's labor? Really think about that. David not only released the plans, but also was willing to release his pocketbook. For many, giving is difficult. Many people assume that God doesn't care about things such as how, why, or what we give. If that were the case, then why was Jesus sitting over against the treasury watching not only WHAT they put in but HOW the rich and a poor widow put their money in the temple treasury in Mark 12:41-42? Why did he say that the widow who gave her last two cents gave more than the others who put much more in if he was not concerned about those details? Why did he say that Cain's offering was not accepted in Genesis 4:5 if all offerings were acceptable in his sight?

I believe Jesus watched how they gave and what they gave in the temple treasury, because giving is a matter of the heart. God always requires his children to tithe or give the first 10 percent of all money that he blesses us with. He also requires us to give beyond the tithe to further his kingdom and help others. However, our motives for giving could keep us from receiving all that God has for us. The beggar who sat at the gate called Beautiful in Acts 3 assumed that Peter and John would give him an exceptional love offering, but instead, he was hit with a bomb. Peter and John told the beggar to look at them. They told this lame man that they did not have silver and gold to give him, but what they did have, he could have. Peter and John told this beggar that if he wanted to walk, then in the name of Jesus, he had to get up and walk. Wow! What a surprise.

Now, if Peter and John had handed the beggar money, how would that have helped him? If Peter and John gave him a one-time monetary offering, he probably would have died a crippled beggar. We should never assume God would have us give money to others, because we may be an enabler for many who refuse to go out and work. Some people assume that the church owes them a living. We need to discern how, what, and to whom he would have us give. Scriptures do tell us we are to help the widows and the fatherless. We do not need to pray about helping them, because the Scriptures tell us to help.

People also assume that because they work a forty-hour week and get a steady paycheck, the money is theirs to spend the way they want. God expects us first to tithe and then pay off our debts and help further His kingdom and help others. I find it very difficult to watch game shows on television that give away thousands and even millions of dollars away to People in many places, when people are starving to death and homeless. It bothers me—and it should bother you. We need to pray and ask God how we can make a difference in the lives of these people.

Second Kings 4:1-7 speaks of a widow who only had a little bit of oil. She was told to gather some empty vessels. When she filled each jar with oil and then sold the oil, she was told first to pay her debts. I have been guilty of not paying my bills first or tithing first. I assumed it was okay to spend what I wanted first and then give God the leftovers. In Matthew 6:9-14 Jesus fed the multitude when the boy gave the only thing he had. When the boy gave what he had to Jesus, Jesus fed the multitude—and then there were leftovers. When you give Jesus the leftovers first, things just don't seem to multiply for you. However, if you give him the first tenth, you will be a part of feeding the multitude—and there will be leftovers. God's principles always work. What would have happened if the lad said no? What would have happened if he said that he could not give, because what he had was not enough to feed a family, let alone more than five thousand people? What if he worried about what would happen to him if he gave all that he had? Mom could have sent him to the market to buy dinner; however, he gave it all with no reservations.

The Word says that we are not our own but that we have been bought with a price. Our money is not our own, either, so stop assuming differently. I remember a time when I had money to go and buy my daughter a new dress. She was a toddler at the time, and buying new clothes for any family member was an extreme struggle. I was caught up on bills, and I went shopping to get her a new dress. I found a beautiful purple dress with lots of ruffles. I took it off the rack and did some more shopping. As I walked through the store, I knew God wanted me to put the dress back. *What? You mean you want me to put the dress back?* That's right! He wanted me to put the dress back up on the rack.

I hate to admit it, but I argued with God right there in the store. I kept saying, "But God, I have the money. It's a beautiful dress. I don't get to do this very often." He instructed me to put the dress back on the rack and then take the money I would have used to buy the dress and buy a tambourine for my friend. She wanted to learn how to play the tambourine for the Lord. I got all the way up to the cash register and was ready to pay for the dress, and God kept saying, *Put it back!* Finally, after much persuasion, I excused myself from the line and put the dress back. Even though I put it back, I was not happy with God at the moment for asking me to do so. I then took the money, went to a Christian bookstore, and purchased a tambourine for my friend.

I came home very upset, but God saw the big picture; I did not. I walked into the living room, and on the couch was a brand new dress just Dawn's size, waiting for me. That dress meant more to me than all the ruffles in the world, because it proved to me that God was in complete control, even though I did not understand. He taught me how he provides for all of our needs—not our wants—when we obey. He may not always provide things the way we want, but he will provide. Abraham said that God would provide a lamb. God didn't provide a lamb for Abraham; instead, God provided a ram. The lamb came two thousand years later, but God did provide a sacrifice for Abraham.

There is nothing wrong with giving, but you can give with a wrong motive that will keep you from receiving God's blessings. Are you giving fifty dollars to receive recognition? Are you giving to receive back? Why are you giving fifty dollars when God said give twenty? That is between you and God. God is looking for obedience more than our money or sacrifices. God wants us to be anxious for nothing but to pray about everything. Does that mean we should pray about what we should give and what we should do? Yes. You don't need to pray about whether you should give 10 percent of your earnings. God clearly states in Malachi 3 that if we do not tithe, then we *rob* God. We fall into the same category as a robber. What happens to a robber when he or she gets caught? The robber may get away with the theft for a season; however, he or she would be locked up in jail if caught. If a robber kept on stealing, he or she could even go to prison. If that happens, the robber would lose all freedom.

Many of us do not receive all of God's blessings, because we are in a prison. We are spiritually locked up, in debt, and do not have enough green stuff to go around. Many of us live from paycheck to paycheck. Many in the United States need plastic surgery. People need to bring out a two-edged sword, which is the word of God, and cut away at their plastic cards. God is not going to do it for you. God wants us to be financially free! Most of us have more going out than coming in and will say we can't afford to give 10 percent of our income. Scripture says in Psalms 121: 8 that God wants to preserve our coming in and our going out. When it comes to receiving a financial blessing, whatever comes in (income) will be protected if what goes out first is the tithe. God blesses obedience. God will not bless disobedience. He will not bless us when we do anything or give anything with wrong motives.

David gave Solomon a pep talk. This, too, can really be tough. Many would struggle to give a word of encouragement when they had the desire, blueprints, and ability to put a plan into action. David spoke encouragement into the life of his son, Solomon. He told Solomon to do the work and be strong. We need to encourage our brothers and sisters in the Lord. The Enemy is out to distract and discourage us. Ask God how you can encourage someone today. However, God may not choose to send people your way to encourage you.

During most of my Christian life, I have had very few people, if any, who encouraged me. Yes, I cried many rivers, but when I look back, I can see God's hand at work in my life. I did not get invited to go many places. Many times, I was overlooked, misunderstood, and criticized. I don't mean to discourage anyone in this chapter, but God may even choose to send many your way to discourage you. Do you disagree with that? Don't put the book down yet. It is biblical. Let us look at some great men of God in the Bible.

In Genesis 37:6,9 it says that Joseph was given dreams. He shared it with his brothers, and his brothers did everything to hinder Joseph's destiny.

Joseph found no encouragement from them, because they envied him. David is another very good example. He was anointed to be king, and Saul did not want to give up his throne. Saul held on very tightly, as we do. Saul did everything in his power to have David assassinated and keep David from the throne. At another time, David had men who walked opposite of him. He was on one side of the road, and they were on the other side. They threw dirt and stones at him. (2 Samuel 16) (Don't ever say you won't take someone's dirt anymore, because God may allow them to pepper you with it.) The Word said David was exhausted, but he made it to his destination.

We are on a journey. Some are on the same side of the road as we are. On the other hand, some are on the opposite side. We will have some opposition along the way, but we can make it church! WE CAN MAKE IT! We may be exhausted, but we can and will make it. Who said it would be easy? No one gave David a pep talk when his wife and children were taken captive. The city of Ziklag was on fire, his own men thought of stoning him, and no one was there to encourage him. However, David encouraged himself in the Lord, his God.(I Samuel 30)

The Devil wants to discourage you. You can read about discouragement from the Enemy in the book of Ezra. Was there ever a time that you withheld encouragement from someone? How many times could you have encouraged someone but did not? Have you considered that you may be experiencing opposition because you gave opposition? We all will reap what we have sown in due time, regardless of how many times we prayed for crop failure. This is something that we need to take into consideration. We are quick to blame the Devil or people when the real problem lies within ourselves. Whether you receive encouragement or not, one thing is certain; God knows how to encourage the discouraged, dismayed, down-and-out, and depressed if we let him.

David prayed as well. Many desire to go as Missionaries, and others would love to give more than they can afford to give. God knows your heart. However, if we cannot go and we cannot give, there is one thing we all can do—*pray*. It is not always convenient or comfortable to pray, but we all can do some kind of praying. We may not feel like praying, especially for those who have been chosen to lead from the blueprints God gave us, but God does require us to pray.

In Acts 9, Ananias assumed he could do more than what God required, and nothing happened. Acts 9 tells the story of Saul's conversion. Both Saul and Ananias were praying. The Lord gave Saul specific directions to get up and go into the city, and *then* he would be told what to do. Saul could not see anything, because he was blind for three days. However, in Damascus was a disciple named Ananias. The Lord called to Ananias in a vision and gave him specific directions concerning where he was to go and what he was to do. All Ananias was told to do was to place his hands on Saul, and Saul's sight would be restored. Ananias was to do nothing more and nothing less (Acts 9:12).

However, as Ananias placed his hands on Saul, he told Saul that God sent him so he could receive a twofold blessing. Ananias told Saul that he would receive his sight and be filled with the Holy Spirit. Jesus never said that; he only said that Saul would receive his sight. Those were the words of Ananias. Saul was not filled with the Holy Spirit when Ananias laid his hands on him. However, Saul did receive his sight. Are you surprised? I am not surprised at all. Did God want Saul to receive the baptism of the Holy Spirit? Yes, but not at that particular time. Being filled with the Holy Spirit would have been great, but it was not God's will at that particular time or place.

We are eager to lay hands on people to receive healings, deliverance, and salvation. The Bible says in I Timothy 5:22 that we are not to lay hands suddenly on anyone. If God told Ananias to lay hands on Saul so that his sight might be restored and he would be filled with the Holy Spirit, both would have happened. I am a firm believer that we will see an outpouring of the Holy Spirit when we all do what God requires of us—nothing more and nothing less. Many times, we go to the altar and start praying for people before praying to God. We then wonder why nothing happens.

I know that is hard to chew—let alone swallow. We put God in a box and think he has to work in a certain way with a certain person, and nothing happens. Listen up, church! Things do not happen as they should, because we do things our way and not God's way. I never rush to the altar to pray for anyone. I don't even like going up front to pray for people if someone asks me to. We need to understand that people at the altar need to be open minded as well. They need to be open and receive prayer from the person God ordains and anoints. I have seen a lot of unhappy campers go home; they are not healed, not delivered, and disappointed, because they wanted God to do things their way. God may not want the pastor or evangelist to pray for them. God may choose a child, a converted prostitute, a converted ex-con, or a converted addict to pray for them—but we are too afraid to turn them loose in our services.

God wants to use each and every one of us. However, we cannot assume it is going to bless God if we all do our own thing any more than it will bless the socks off me if my kids do their own thing. Nothing will happen until we are in line with God's will and God's Word. What does God want you to do? Is it God's will that you be healed and filled with the Holy Spirit? Yes, it is God's will. It will happen when you are in a right relationship with the Lord. Allow God to use others if he chooses, and do only the things he wants you to do. Much of the time, we do not allow God to use others. Pride, anger, resentment, and jealousy are imbedded deep within us. We need to stop thinking that it's all about us. I am not saying you can't pray for people, because God's Word tells us to pray for others, but praying with results requires obedience.

David prayed and fought the Philistines. He was victorious, because he prayed. God gave him the battle plan, and when he obeyed, he was victorious. After a matter of time, the Philistines showed their ugly heads again. What did David do? Of course, he fought the battle the same way he fought it before, because that plan had worked for him. David had better sense than that. He could have assumed that if he won the battle a certain way before, he should fight the same way again. However, David did not *assume*; he prayed and then prayed again. God gave him a variety of specific directions to follow. When he did what God wanted him to do, he got victory again and again. Get the battle plan straight from the captain himself.

David did things a certain way the first time, but he prayed first. However, he was not meant to do things that way again. He had to always inquire of the Lord. He had to stop, pray, listen, and then do what God said. He always received fresh, new direction when he gained victory over the Philistines. People like comfort zones.

In my Sunday school class, my teacher said that the Holy Spirit will lead us to places that take us out of our comfort zones, but that is why the Holy Spirit is called our comforter. People like the familiar (including myself). People go by the direction of a book they have read or the advice of others who have walked where they want to walk. Answers to prayer and miracles can only happen as you pray and follow the leading of the Holy Spirit. Everybody has different ideas on prayer. Who is right? Everyone who writes or teaches us about prayer is probably right. Their experiences were right for them, but that does not mean that they will be right for us. It was right for them, because that is the direction God took them.

We are talking about a relationship. Not everyone will do it the same way. God's battle plan to deliver me from smoking was not the same battle plan God had for my husband. God specifically told my husband to lay his cigarettes on the altar, and he was delivered. I ran out to the car to get my cigarettes and laid them on the altar, and nothing happened until years later. I was delivered a different way. Seek God, ask God, listen to God, and then do what he says for *you* to do, not what an author or television evangelist tells you to do. You can't go wrong. Otherwise, you will become confused.

It is great to hear testimonies of what God has done for others. He *can* do the same for us when we start doing what he wants. People also become confused when different people prophesy over them. That happened to me. I was always expecting a man or woman to call me out of my pew and give me a prophetic word so I would know what direction I was to take. It is much easier to hear people give me direction than to get on my face before Almighty God and hear for myself. God let me know a few years ago that he gave me exactly what I wanted. He said, "I gave you what you wanted. You wanted someone to call you out of your seat and give you a word." Then God dropped the bomb: *"But was it my Word?"* That hit me in the core of my being. What has God said to you? Do you believe what God has spoken to you in prayer? You need to seek and be still, and then you will see the salvation of the Lord.

In closing this chapter lets look at other examples when
people assumed they could do things their way:

-Reading 2 Chronicles 26:16-21 Uzziah was a powerful man as long as he sought the Lord. However, he assumed he could go before the altar of incense and burn incense. Azariah, the priest, and eighty others followed Uzziah and confronted him. They told him that what he was doing was wrong. He chose to follow what he assumed was okay and became angry, and God afflicted him with leprosy until the day he died.

-2 Samuel 6:3-8 David became very angry with the Lord, because the Lord smote Uzzah for trying to steady the Ark. David could have assumed that because it was falling, it was right for them to try to keep that from happening. However, God gave specific instructions as to how the Ark was to be carried and by whom. If they did it God's way, it would not have fallen in the first place. If we take God and His Word more seriously and do things his way, we will not stumble either.

Never assume anything. Your assumption could cost your life and the lives of others. We can be guaranteed of victory when we do things God's way and not our way. There is no other way!

Prayer: Father, I come to you to confess my sin of assumption. I know that many times, I have had desires to do spiritual activities, and I assumed you would be pleased. After reading about David, I have come to realize that even though you may give us a blueprint on what and how some things are to be done, we must seek your face, be still before you, and hear what you want us to do with what you show us. Just as you said no to David, you may choose to say no to me. Give me your strength and discernment to release, give, and do all that you require of me. In Jesus name – Amen!

Time To Reflect

1. Are you *called* into ministry, or do you *assume* it is okay to pursue a ministry because it is a spiritual activity?

2. Has the Holy Spirit given you a blueprint for a certain ministry?

3. When the Holy Spirit reveals a plan to you, do you feel you must see it through, or do you continue praying and ask God for divine direction as to what he would have you do with the plans he showed you?

4. What has God revealed to you? Remember, David was given the blueprint of the temple by the Holy Spirit, but his son, Solomon, was meant to build the temple.

5. If God gave you a blueprint for a specific ministry as well as the ability to see it through, would you have a difficult time releasing it to another person, as David did to his son? Why or why not? Search your heart, and be honest.

6. Are you an encourager to those who have the same talent as you do? For example, if you have a gift and a desire to teach a Sunday School class but someone else is called upon, can you give a word of encouragement to that person?

7. Are you willing to give to see God's kingdom built even if you can't lead? Can you pray for those who build, lead, teach, and preach when you feel you should do what they are doing?

8. Do you believe God has a specific plan for your life?

9. Why do you think God tells us *no* when we have both the desire and the ability to see a plan through?

chapter 6

Afraid To Say No

I have been guilty of not being able to say no many times. I just do not know how to say *no!* Titus 2:11-12 tells us that God's grace teaches us to say that nasty, two-letter word. Trust me when I say that God's grace teaches us to say no. He has had to teach me that saying no is okay.

When I am asked to do something, I really want to say no, but I feel like I have a sock in my mouth, and the word just won't come out. Instead, I quickly say, "Sure, I'll do it; no problem. I can even do this, if you would like." Then the pressure is on. I beat my head and say, "Why did I do that?" Been there, done that, right? If God can say no, then why can't I? If others can say no, then why can't I? God teaches us that *no* is an okay word to use. By his grace, he teaches us to say no.

Don't you find some people kind of funny? Really, I find them hilarious—extremely hilarious. When I shared with people how tired or busy I was, they would tell me how I needed to slow down. So I did. Guess what happened? Can you believe that some got a little perturbed with me? They wanted me to slow down and start saying no to people, but they did not want me to say no to them. Have you been there? I thought so! Someone always ended up getting mad. Have you ever considered that when you cannot say no, you might rob others of a blessing? God may raise other people—or a whole new generation— and equip them for service. Are we willing to pass the baton—or the mantle, as Elijah did to Elisha as in I Kings 19:19?

I totally understand why Scripture tells us that God's grace teaches us to say *no*. It does not come easy for many of us. The ability to say the word *no* is taught by the Holy Spirit. Some of us, such as myself, are taught to say no by hard knocks. This skill is taught by disappointment, heartache, and sorrow. It is taught when we start feeling fatigued and run-down. It is taught when you are hurt, because no one hears you anymore. God allows others not to hear you to slow you down.

Yes, only God's grace *teaches* us to say this two-letter word. Saying no is not only for busyness. You can say no to a second helping of food, to using the credit card, or when you know you are ready to enter a bad relationship. It can apply to many areas of our lives. What part of *no* don't you understand? I have learned that what was once a nasty word has become one of my favorite words in the English language. Since writing this chapter, I have told two people that I am dropping out of two ministries I feel God has not called me to help out, and I feel good about it! *Hooray for me!*

I think many people are afraid to say no. Saying no can be one of the biggest reasons people choose to stay so busy. What are we afraid of? There are all kinds of fears. We may fear old age, standing in front of others, rejection, failure, heights, water, traveling, dogs, and mice. The list of fears can go on and on. Who and/or what are we afraid of? Some fear crowds, and others are afraid to talk to others one-on-one.

Elijah challenged 450 prophets of Baal to worship and serve the one true God, but when it came to *one woman*, Jezebel, he was afraid and ran for his life. He ran to save his life, but on the flip side of the coin, he sat down under a broom tree and prayed that he might die. It sounds like he was afraid to live and afraid to die. Fear is a terrible thing. Those who walked with Jesus day after day had fear. Many times, Jesus told those who walked closest to him not to be afraid. The words "fear not or don't be afraid" appear at least 365 times in the Bible—one "fear not" for each day of the year.

Deuteronomy 2:10 tells us about the Emimites. The Emimites were a strong and numerous people as tall as the Anakites. They were considered to be *giants!* The "Emimites" have to do with *fear, terror, horror,* or *fright.* Fear or being afraid is a giant that many of us can relate to but *must* overcome. In order to possess the land, we must drive out the previous occupants of fear and go in and occupy in their place.

David was not afraid to meet Goliath head-on. The Word says in I Samuel 17:22, 48 that David ran toward the giant, not away from him. Hey, you can stop avoiding people because you are afraid. "Who, me, afraid of people?" you ask. Yes, you are afraid that if they ask you to do something, you will be afraid to say no. I can recall a grown man hiding between the wall and his refrigerator, because he was afraid to say no. It makes me laugh every time I think of it. (Don't tell anyone, but it was my husband.) It is much easier to run away from or shun people then it is to run or walk toward them and say to them, "Thanks for asking me, but no thanks!" David ran and met Goliath.

Let's take a look at 1 Samuel 17. David was a champion! I believe that in order to be a champion in God's army, you must be willing and able to say both *yes* and *no*. If we do not know how to say no, we will be so drained that we will no longer have strength to stand against the Enemy. When you know you are anointed, God will give you the ability. He will equip, enable, and empower you to accomplish what he has called you to do. Sometimes it takes all of God's strength just to say no. We need to know when God wants us to say yes and when he wants us to say no.

We are afraid to say no; yet David said yes to taking on a challenge and then was accused when he wanted to knock Goliath's block off. Why—or better yet, who—would want to accuse David because he wanted to kill the giant, Goliath? First Samuel 16:13 gives a hint as to both who and why. Among David's audience when he was anointed were his older brothers. David was chosen, and his brothers were rejected. From that day on, the Spirit of the Lord was upon David in *power!* David could have said *no* and ran away from the giant, but instead, he chose to meet Goliath head-on. Saying *yes* to the challenge only annoyed his brothers.

David's brothers were annoyed by at least four things—the anointing on his life, his abilities, his appearance, and the blessed assurance he had in God to do whatever God wanted him to do. Because of this, David's brother's accused him of several things. *What on earth can they accuse us of?* Have you ever said no and been accused of being lazy? Have you been accused of being in your comfort zone, being complacent, or just not caring? There will be people who dislike you for not only saying no to them, but also for saying yes to a challenge. Some people may get mad if you say yes, because they are jealous of your anointing or your God-given talents, abilities, or gifts. David's brothers were definitely jealous. They admired what David possessed but abhorred David himself, because they did not have the same character and courage that David was blessed with.

We must have discernment to know when to say yes and when to say no. David was not only anointed to meet the challenge, but also to press through the jealousies and accusations against him for doing what he knew God wanted him to do. However, if you are not anointed, you will *not* have the same assurance that David had.

David was accused of having a wicked heart. His heart was not wicked. David knew there was a cause. When you know there is a cause, you will not be afraid to do what God tells you to do, even if he tells you to just say no. The King James Version tells us in I Samuel 17:29 that David said to his brothers, "Is there not a cause?" David could say yes to killing the giant, because he knew there was a cause. Telling others no could be a giant that some people might find challenging in their walk with the Lord. David used five small stones to kill the giant, but he only needed one of the five to knock him dead. God wants you to overcome the giant in your life. Some of us may kill a giant with only one stone—a two-letter word—*no!*

David knew that Goliath was defying the armies of the living God, and he wanted to remove the disgrace from Israel. Many people look at this portion of Scripture and assume that David met the challenge because of the reward involved. It is very true that David would be the son-in-law of the king. He would reap great benefits if he met the challenge. However, I believe David's motives went beyond the reward. David said he wanted to see the disgrace removed from Israel, and he wanted Goliath, the uncircumcised Philistine who was defying the armies of the living God, to be removed as well.

David did not say no to the challenge—so how does this apply to your life? Have you ever considered that God may want you to say no to some activities in your life? If you pursue and do what you or others want you to do, then you, like Goliath, are defying the true and living God. You are resisting *his authority*. How do parents feel when they want their children to do (or not do) something? If children go against what their parents tell them, then aren't they defying or resisting the parents' authority? It does not make parents happy, and I am positive that it does not make the Lord happy, either. When others want you to do anything—even if it is a spiritual task—and you know God does not want you to do it but do it anyway because you cannot say no, then you are resisting his authority. You are defying the true and living God.

There is a cause for saying no as well as a cause to saying yes. The cause may be God teaching us obedience. God may be teaching us to have patience and wait on him. God could be raising others to step up to the plate. Stepping up to the plate can have tremendous consequences if you are not careful. God could also be teaching us to lay our Issac's on the altar as Abraham did in Genesis 22. God may be teaching us to rest. Did you ever think you might need some time to rest, relax, be revived, rejuvenate, and be refreshed?

In 1 Samuel 17:29, David asked what he had done. I can really relate to David. When you say no to some people, they can give you a guilt trip for saying no. They will make you think you have committed an unpardonable sin. It's not always easy to stand up for yourself when you know that saying no is the right thing to do. People wanted me to slow down, take it easy, and learn to say no. I wasn't sure if I could actually say no without angering or upsetting anyone. If there is one thing I hate, and that is to have a guilt trip put on me. The Lord let me know that I was a person who was riddled with guilt. People would tell me that I could say no, but then they would proceed to tell me how they were asked to be in charge of a committee but then could not because of this and that and another. Then relatives were coming to pay them a visit, and then they would expect me to rescue them by taking on the responsibility and do what they were supposed to do. If they prayed first, God knew these people would not or could not keep their commitments.

God knows the future. If you pray, he will answer you—yes or no. God knows that if you say yes, you are not going to be able to keep a commitment on a certain day, because something else will come up—a funeral, wedding, family issues, or family plans. I can't tell you how many times I said yes to something a month away before praying, and then when that day came, my husband had plans, and I felt trapped, because I made a commitment at church. The guilt could have been avoided if I had said, "Let me pray first, and then I will get back with you." Pray first. Listen for God's answer.

Psalm 100 says that we are to serve the Lord with gladness. I hate to admit this, but I have been anything but glad when I got a call to do something that somebody else committed to. How can anyone enter God's gates with thanksgiving and his courts with praise if he or she is burnt out? Instead of praise and thanksgiving, we will come with griping, complaining, fatigue, and weariness.

Saying no to people can be a terrifying experience. Some will accuse us of being lazy and complacent while others may carry attitudes toward you, but that's okay. Others will admire your strength and courage to say no. Does it really matter what others think? Of course it does not matter what they think.

Take a look at what happened to Aaron in Exodus 32 because he could not say no. Aaron was a people-pleaser; he wanted to please the crowd. Moses took a long time coming down from the mountain. Aaron was experiencing peer pressure at the foot of the mountain, because it was taking Moses so long to come down. The people kept demanding that Aaron make them gods. Aaron could have said, "No, I don't think so," but he didn't. Instead, Aaron said, "Okay, you want gods; I will give you gods. Break off your earrings." This caused Aaron to lead the people into idolatry—and then he lied when he was confronted. For a workaholic—especially those who are people-pleasers—staying idle can be dangerous. Because of their compulsion to be doing something—especially if there motive is to please— they can easily start building golden idols and can and will lead others in idolatry. While Moses received the Law, Aaron broke the law. He put the golden calf before God, and then he lied. Can you believe he said, "Out came this golden calf?" (see Exodus 32)

Are we where God wants us? Are we doing what God wants or what everybody else wants because we are afraid to say no? If God does not place us where we are, we do not please him. He is the only one who we have to please. It is okay to say no. If God can say no, so can we. As a matter of fact, if we fear God, then we better say no to the things God does not want us to do. The fear of God will keep us from sin or disobedience. His grace will continually teach us to say *no*—not only to ungodliness and worldly passions, but also to live a self-controlled life. In order to do that, we must learn to say no if God does not call—even if the activity is spiritual. For some, this will not be an easy task.

Some of us seem to think that saying no only pertains to immorality. God is asking us to say no to some activities that we take on ourselves. He does not want us to be tired and fatigued. Many times, we are drained, because we bite off more than we can chew. Again, I am not saying you can't help out in the nursery, help with dinners, or clean the church. I am not saying you can't say yes to helping out with Sunday school. I am talking about people who are out of balance because they can't say no.

In I Samuel 17:17-20 Jesse, David's father told David to take an ephah of parched corn and ten loaves and run to the camp to his brothers. David left the sheep with a keeper and did as his father had commanded him. While he was there with his brothers, it said in verse 28 that his brother Eliab was angry with David and asked him why he came down and who did he leave the sheep with. David was accused of being a spectator. He was told that he only came to watch the battle. This is something that others will definitely accuse you of if you say no. You are either in the race or a spectator. Some seem to think if we are not doing, then we are not in the race. It can appear that we're mere spectators if we are not doing what people expect us to be doing. What will people think of us?

I mentioned playing baseball. You are in the ball game, in the bleachers, or on the bench as a spectator. Did you know that you and I could be responsible for forfeiting a game by breaking the rules? If God does not want me in the ball game and I am still determined to pursue it, then I broke the rules. If God wants me in the game and I choose to be a spectator, I break the rules; therefore, I forfeit the game. If I come to church dinners after everyone has worked hard to contribute, cook, and clean, God just might choose for me to sit and do absolutely nothing for a change. We should be able to do that without feeling any guilt if God wants us to rest for once.

I am not saying you can never help; we are dealing with motives in this book. If you are one who is always helping with the church dinners, cleaning the church, serving on the cleanup committee, working in the children's department, and teaching children's church, then you might have to put your foot down, tell people no, and start being a spectator for once. Maybe it's time to give someone else the cleaning sponge so you can become a sponge in the presence of God Almighty. Let someone else do the work for once. They may not understand and get mad, but that is fine and dandy. Let them think what they want to think. *I know it won't be easy, but you can do this.*

I know it is not easy to be misunderstood. Many in the Bible were very misunderstood. The mother of Jesus was a prime example. Can you imagine telling your parents that you were pregnant even though you said no to a man? (Not that Joseph asked.) What about Joseph, who told his brothers that one day, they and his parents would bow down to him? You are not going to be very popular! Remember, God has not called us to be popular; he has called us to be obedient. You might be hated, spit upon, locked up, and even called a crazy lunatic, but that is okay. If God is for us, then who or what can be against us?

I cannot stress the importance of obedience enough—even if obeying God means telling a few people, "Thanks, but no thanks." Some people may not think that this is an issue to consider at all. Yes, you might be accused of being a spectator who sits and watches while everybody else does things, but that's okay. We all know that Jesus only did what he saw the Father do, and he only said things he heard from his Father. Do you think the Father expects anything different from us? We know that we are to follow in Jesus' footsteps. We are to be imitators of him—even if it means being a spectator occasionally. If he only did the things that his Father expected, then we must do the same.

Prayer: Father God, I come to you, admitting that it is very hard for me to say no to people. I worry that people won't like me if I tell them no. I also feel that I must do something when it seems like you are taking a long time to do what you are supposed to do. Help me to be still and wait on you and your timing. Let me know what I am to do, when I am to speak, and when I am to be still and do nothing. I need your discernment. I need your help. In Jesus name – Amen!

Time To Reflect

1. Are you afraid to say no to people? Why or why not?

2. Have you ever been accused of being complacent, staying in your comfort zone, or not caring because you said no? How did it make you feel?

3. What were some of the accusations that David had to face when saying *yes* to the challenge of facing and killing the giant, Goliath?

4. Have some of the accusations that David faced kept you from saying yes or no and becoming a champion for God?

5. Has God told you to say no to a ministry or some activity?

6. Have you felt the pressure of others wanting you to pursue something that God said you should not do? Why would you still pursue the ministry or the activity if God said no? What are you doing to God's authority?

7. How do parents feel when they tell their kids no, and the children continue to do what they want anyhow? What are they doing to both God's and their parents' authority?

chapter 7

Avoiding Emotional Pain

The subject of abuse is starting to come further out of the closet as the years go by. This type of pain has crippled young and old alike. It has disabled boys and girls as well as men and women. It has caused many to be committed to psychiatric wards, withdraw from society, or distrust everyone. Some have even committed suicide.

We hear about women and children going through physical, sexual, or emotional abuse, but we very seldom hear about men who have been sexually abused by a father, brother, uncle, cousin, or even a woman. At my annual staff meeting, a sergeant came to talk to my coworkers and me. He was the first person I have ever heard mention a man being raped. It does not matter if we hear about it or not; the fact remains that even men have been and will be sexually abused. No one is exempt these days.

You will read in 2 Samuel 13 about Tamar who was raped by her half-brother, Amnon. Absolom told her to be quiet, because Amnon was her brother. *Stuff your pain,* in other words. I wonder how many adults and children have been told to be quiet after being molested, abused, or raped. *Hush* is the word. *Don't tell anyone that this happened to you.* Many have even been threatened if they dare to speak up and tell anyone what has happened to them. Absolom not only told Tamar to be quiet, but also was very insensitive when he told her not to take it to heart. (I desperately want to call him a jerk—I guess I just did!) Some believed the lies their predators told them and took their secret shame to the grave. People who have been abused have a tendency to sweep their abuse under the carpet; but the truth is that their secret goes much deeper than that. They carry their shame and pain for many long and painful years.

I taught a women's group and mentioned the shepherds who tended their flocks when the Christ child was born. The shepherds were told not to be afraid when the glory of the Lord shone round about them. I thought, *"Why would they be afraid?"* And they were not afraid; they were terrified! Why would any us be afraid to be in God's presence? Would you be?

I have come to the conclusion that silence can be quite intimidating. I believe one reason so many of us are afraid to be still in God's presence is because he just might show up. Listen up! When we are in his presence, we are privileged to hear his voice. Yes, it is a privilege to hear him. When we hear his voice, he is not talking to our spouse, our children, or our brothers or sisters in Christ. He is not even talking to the pastor at the moment. When he talks to you, he is talking only to you! He will not talk to you about anyone else unless he tells you to pray for them. He will talk to you about *you!* That can be a little scary. So what is the big deal? The problem is not that God will talk to us but that what he has to say can be terrifying. There is responsibility that comes with hearing his voice. What will we do with what we hear him say to us?

I know that I should read the Word and pray every day. I have no problem getting out of bed, walking downstairs, and doing that. However, it is those times when I know God is specifically leading me to spend time with him, I truly struggle. I feel that he leads, because he wants to show me something about myself. I get a gut feeling that I am not going to like what he has to say. His words could even be a little painful and uncomfortable. The healing process is not always pleasant.

There was a time when I knew God was leading me to read his Word. I knew he wanted to speak to me. I sat down and opened my Bible to where I had left off the day before. Everything was fine until he started to show me something about myself that was quite painful. I got out of the chair and it was like his hand touched the top of my head. I knew that he wanted me to sit down, because he was not finished with me yet. I could even picture him clearing his throat before speaking to me. I definitely sat back down and let him do the work he wanted to do.

God wants an intimate relationship with us. Intimacy with him will not happen with just a touch here and there. He is a perfect gentleman. He will not force himself on anyone. God wants to *make* us free, according to the King James Version. He did not say in John 8 that he would set us free but that he would make us free. It is a process. If he sets us free, it is instantaneous. There are some areas of your life that he might set you free in an instant. However, when he makes us free, it is a process—and sometimes the process is painful and uncomfortable.

First Corinthians 2:10 states how the Spirit *searches all things—even the deep things of God.* The Spirit searches even the things that we have buried deep. We work very hard to avoid emotional pain. We work overtime and have a funeral, burying our pain—but we are burying it under the wrong things. We have buried our pain very deep in the "dirt of works." In other words we find work to do to bury our pain. Others bury pain with substance abuse, cutting and etc.

The Spirit not only searches, but also brings the things that we have buried deep in our hearts to the surface. When God deals with me and tells me to be still, I know that he wants to speak life and freedom into my life. However, I can get quite antsy. As a friend of mine says, "Pastor sure made us squirm in our seats this morning." I don't get this antsy feeling when I am just going through the motions of Bible reading, devotions, and prayer—only when God is leading. It is then that I can find all kinds of things to *do.* The reason for this is very simple. If I stay busy, then I won't have to go before Jesus, the Great Physician, for physical or emotional healing. I do my best to avoid pain. I hate pain!

Let's look at some major reasons people do not go to a physical doctor when they experience symptoms or have pain and then relate that experience in the Spirit. The first reason is time. We always use time as the excuse to not do things we know we should do. We have time to watch television, talk on the telephone, and e-mail friends, but when it comes to taking the time to read the Word and pray or go to the doctor, we say we do not have time. We make sure we find the time to do things we like.

Second, we are fearful of what we might find out. When we go before the Lord, he can reveal why we have pain and discomfort. He is able to pinpoint exactly what the problem is. Sometimes the doctor may have to run a few tests on us to make the proper diagnosis. It is then that things show up. Things that have been buried deep for years seem to come to the surface when circumstances are ripe. A good example might be anger. You may feel like you are free from anger until someone does something to you and you realize then that you still have anger.

Third, some seem to think that their problems will go away. Years ago, I had severe heartburn. I always felt like an apple was stuck in the middle of my stomach. I did not want to go see my family doctor, because I was terrified of having some kind of stomach cancer. However, I knew I had to make the move. Finally, after much suffering, I got the nerve to go. I got the phone book, looked up the number, and made the phone call. I sat in the waiting room, petrified of what might be. The television played health programs, and it kept me somewhat relaxed. After waiting for a time, I went in, was weighed, and had my vital signs read. After that was finished, I had another long wait.

Let me give you some good advice—if you are in a big hurry, bring a good book that you really desire to read. If I bring my book, then I always seem to get out early. If I do not bring my book, then I will sit on the patient bed and stare at all the pictures on the wall. The first time I was at the doctor's office, I did not have a book of any kind. All I could do was read what was on the wall. One sign ministered to me as I read it. It said, "The five most dangerous words are *maybe it will go away.*" Maybe it will, but what if it doesn't? What if something is wrong with you and you don't even know it? I can guarantee that if something is wrong with you and you don't know it, you cannot be given the proper treatment.

Fourth, we may not like what the doctor prescribes any more than Naaman liked what he was told to do if he wanted to be healed of his leprous condition in 2 Kings the 5th chapter. He had to wash in muddy Jordan—which brought more pain—before healing took place. Sometimes the doctor will tell us to take medicine only as needed. However, there are times when the doctor will ask you to take all of the medicine until it is gone. When my children were young, I did not know this. I learned this as a grandmother. If you do not take the medicine until it is completely gone, there is a good chance of catching what you had all over again. The same principle applies to spiritual things.

Naaman was told he had to go wash—not once, but seven times. God did not tell Naaman to wash only when needed. He did not tell Naaman to wash once or twice and then quit if he felt better. No, God told Naaman he had to wash seven complete times in the Jordan. When Naaman did, he came out of the water as clean as a baby, and his condition never came back again. There are certain things that will keep coming back if you do not do things God's way. He may tell you that if you really want to be healed, all you need to do is eat healthier, quit smoking, avoid alcohol, drink more water, exercise, and get more rest. The good doctor may even tell you to cut back on some activities. You know, maybe you are too busy. Jesus may tell us that in order to be healed, we need to forgive someone, repent, and make things right. I believe that when God heals, he wants to heal completely so the issue never comes back again. Can it be that some do not follow the directions the Great Physician prescribes? They begin to feel the bitter pain again.

People don't want to come to the Lord for healing, because they might come to realize that something is wrong with them and not with others. The problem usually is with the self, not others. There will be times when we will hurt because of something someone else has done to us emotionally or physically. However, the pain should not linger forever. If someone did hurt us, we need to forgive to be healed. When we go to the Great Physician, we will find that sometimes the problem lies within us if we continue to hold on to bitterness and are not able to forgive. Regardless of what others may have done to us, we need to forgive. I am learning worry can hinder us from being healed as well.

What if we avoid going to the doctor because we are afraid the physician will tell us that we have cancer? If we don't go, we won't know. However, if we do know, the healing can take place with the proper medication, treatment, and time. It is the same in the spiritual realm. We must come before the Great Physician and then let him give us the diagnosis. We must let him give us the proper treatment so that we might be healed. I have a terrible habit of trying to tell my doctor what I think is wrong with me. We try to tell God what is wrong with us, too. Come on, fess up. "I'm not lazy; I'm just a little tired today." "Angry—who me? I'm not angry; I'm just frustrated." "I'm just having a bad day."

If I want to get better, I need to shut up, let God examine me, and let him give the report. God is faithful to show us if we will ask. I always pray that God will show me my heart as he sees it. There are some days when we do not want to look in the mirror. We sometimes fear coming to the mirror of God's Word and seeing our wrinkles, blemishes, and spots. However, I can see a lot of *your* wrinkles, blemishes, and spots, but not my own. The problem is not so much in seeing them but what are we going to do about them.

If you want to get a wrinkle out of a garment, you have to apply some heat and pressure. If you want to get a blemish to go away, as painful as it might be, you have to squeeze it. Do you have a spot? Some spots take lots of elbow grease to remove. For any of these things to go away, you will experience some kind of pain. When the heat, pressure, or squeeze is on, you won't laugh. Come on, church. God is looking for a church without spots, blemishes, or wrinkles. Let he who started a good work in us complete that work—regardless of how painful it might get. Stop being so busy that you ignore going to Jesus.

Prayer: Father God, I have been working overtime to avoid emotional pain. I am carrying a lot of pain, shame, guilt, and condemnation, because I was abused. I need to forgive my abuser for what he/she did to me. Help me to see my heart as you see it. Show me what I must do to be healed. God, I want you to not only touch me, but also penetrate my heart. I want to be transformed and conformed into your image and likeness. In Jesus name – Amen!

Time To Reflect

1. Tamar was told to stay quiet and not to take it to heart when Amnon raped her. Do you carry shame around with you like a ball and chain because someone has told you to stay quiet? Be honest.

2. If you carry guilt and shame, what are you going to do about it? Were you told not to take it to heart, as Tamar was? How did that make you feel?

3. Do you struggle with being still before the Lord? If so, why?

4. Are you afraid of what God may say to you?

5. What brings pain and discomfort to you?

6. Do you want God to only touch you, or do you want to be transformed by letting him penetrate your heart?

7. What keeps you from letting God into every area of your life?

8. You may have God, but in all honesty, does he have all of *you*?

9. If you were to go before the Great Physician, what do you think the diagnosis would be?

10. If God tells you that you have a problem, would you be willing to accept it, or would you be in denial?

We can trust that God loves us—even in our deepest pain. He knows what is best for us, and he wants to heal every area of our lives. There are times when the healing process can be painful, but we must trust that God will bring us through it.

chapter 8

Why The Devil Wants To Keep You Busy

We are now going into the second half of the book. This section deals with the reasons the Devil wants to keep you and me busy. It makes me understand more clearly why Pharoah was so concerned about Moses and Aaron trying to get the people of Israel to stop working. The Devil has many ways of keeping us from being all that God wants us to be. If he can't keep us angry, offended, unforgiving, or selfish, then he will keep us busy and burnt out. They say there is nothing any colder than ashes after the fire has gone out. The ashes need to be stoked or fanned and the fire rekindled. Years ago, I taught a message to a youth group in Texas entitled, "Why the Fire?" In Matthew 3:11 John said "I indeed baptize you with water unto repentance: but he that cometh after me is mightier than I, whose shoes I am not worthy to bear; he shall baptize you with the Holy Ghost, and with fire." If you ever understood the purpose of fire, you will then understand better why the Devil wants you burnt out. He wants to put out the fire of the Holy Ghost in your life. Fire brings warmth. Fire changes the form of things. Fire can melt the thickest block of ice to a puddle or pool of water.

Fire also purges. Fire can give light. Fire can destroy. There are things in our lives that we need the fire of the Holy Ghost to destroy.

Fire can tenderize food. Put lasagna or macaroni noodles in boiling water, and they become tender. Fire can also harden. There are things in our lives that God needs to tenderize. There are also things in our lives that God needs to solidify. Fire can bring out the aroma of whatever is cooking over a stove or in an oven. If given the choice between instant oatmeal or pudding and cooked oatmeal or pudding, I want the food cooked over a fire. Just talking about it makes me want to go cook some pudding right now. Fire can also weld metal.

My friend, Ruth, told me how God spoke prophetically to her. She then told me great things that God had spoken to her. One day, I prayed and asked God why he did not speak prophetically to me as he did to her. I envied her and wanted the same prophetic experience she had. I will never forget the words He said to me: "You have not chosen me, but I have chosen you. I have chosen you in the furnace of affliction [ouch]. Be like Moses, choosing to suffer affliction with the people of God [double ouch] than to enjoy the pleasures of sin for a season. Choose ye this day whom you will serve."

Wow—the words came prophetically and quite fast. No thinking about that one. I chewed on God's words for a while and noticed a theme. I began to see the words *choose, chose,* and *chosen*. When I looked up the word *chosen* in *Strong's Exhaustive Concordance*, I noticed the word *join*. For some reason, just out of the blue, I asked my husband how one welds. What happens when you weld? He said that welding took much heat. The heat is what holds the metals together. Fire, my friend, is needed in our walk so we can grow. If we want to become one with God, we must go through the fire. He told me that day that he had chosen me in the furnace of affliction.

Furnaces are hot. How many times have we heard that when it gets *hot* in the kitchen, we need to get out? This is not true; that is a time to stay—to abide, to remain. God is in the process of joining, welding, and making us one with him. God also does this in our relationships—especially in marriages. Many divorces happen because the spouses just can't take the heat.

Just think what might have happened if Noah got out of the ark before God told him to come out. Noah took the top off the ark and looked around. Oh, the smell of the outdoors. We must remember that he was in the ark for at least a year with a wife, his children, his in-laws, and animals. The Bible does not say that there were conflicts, but I am sure there were. The women were in the ark for at least a year. There might have been tension from PMS or menopause. Noah was on the inside looking out, and I think he liked what he saw. The Word says, "The ground appeared dry, but only on the surface." It would have been a cinch to leave the ark before God wanted Noah to do so. However, Noah chose to remain—to abide in the ark until God told him to come out.

Sometimes we are on the outside looking in, but Noah was on the inside looking out. I am sure he was tempted to come on down, but the price would not have been right. His whole household was saved, because he chose to obey God from the time he was told to build the ark to the time he came out of the ark.

If you read Acts 27:31The apostle Paul, as well as his men, had to abide in the ship if they were going to be safe from the storm. They had a choice to jump on the lifeboat or abide in the ship. Paul decided that they were to cut the ties that were holding the lifeboat to the ship. God told me that I needed to cut the ties to everything that felt safe to me. We don't want to leave our comfort zone or our safety nets. Leaving the ship would have seemed like the right thing to do if the disciples were going to be safe, but instead, Paul told them that they had to cut the ties to all security and safety and remain in the ship, regardless of what it looked like if they were going to be saved. This was not easy!

Before food can be added to a pan, the pan must be greased or oiled. The Word talks about the oil of gladness. (Psalms 45:7) When God is telling us to remain in fiery situations, without this oil, we will not be able to withstand the fire that is so desperately needed in our lives. Without this oil in a pan before it goes through the fire, substances will stick on so badly that you will either have to scrub for hours, trying to get it off, or discard the pan. This happens to many people. The heat is on, but they don't have the oil of gladness, and they don't know how to handle the heat. Attitudes, bitterness, and resentment will begin to stick to us. These things are repulsive. Their efforts are then good for nothing. These people end up getting spiritually stuck or are discarded.

I was helping with a chicken and biscuit dinner at church, cleaning up and washing dishes. As I washed dishes, I came to a pan that had turned black at the bottom. I began scrubbing, and it seemed like I was getting nowhere. I felt it was hopeless. Then I decided to let it soak for a bit in some hot, soapy water. *That's a smart move!* I thought. I continued to wash the rest of the dishes and then came back to the dirty pan. I noticed that after it soaked a bit, the food that had been burned and stuck on fell right off.

A revelation hit me. *That is it!* It is amazing how God can give us revelations while we do menial tasks if we stay in tune with him. We try very hard in our own strength to come clean. Instead, God told me that if I want to come clean in the areas that I feel stuck in, then I need to sit and soak in his Word and his presence. As we soak in these things, then our attitudes and resentments will begin to fall off of us.

Let me make one thing clear, though; God does not discard any one. Condemnation is not from the Lord! People condemn themselves so badly that they discard themselves and keep themselves from being all that God wants them to be. They give up and then quit. The Devil wants us to quit, but God wants us to press on to the finish line. Get on fire for God. Be baptized with the Holy Ghost and *fire,* and never let the Devil put out your fire by keeping you busy to the point of burnout. Receive the oil of the Holy Spirit—the oil of gladness—when you know God requires you to remain in circumstances that you are enduring. Have the discernment and knowledge to know when to remain and when to relinquish. The Enemy is slick and sly, and he knows what he is doing. He will do everything he can to keep you busy.

Prayer: Father, I have been so busy that the fire has been extinguished. I ask that you set my heart on fire once again with a love and passion to do only the things you want me to do. Baptize me with the Holy Ghost and fire. I need that fire to melt away the things that need to be melted and harden the things that need hardening. I need the oil of gladness so when fiery trials come my way I won't have bad attitudes sticking to me but I will offer up the sacrifices of praise and thanksgiving instead unto you. Open my eyes so I understand that I need fire to purify me. Make me one with you, and make me one with others in relationships that you want me to be in. In Jesus name- Amen!

We need to burn bright, not burn out.

Time To Reflect

1. What are some things that have kept you busy and burnt out?
2. Why do we need to be baptized with the Holy Ghost and fire?
3. If you want to become one with God or one with your spouse, what is necessary in your spiritual life?
4. What kind of oil do we need when we go through the refining fires of life?
5. What does God expect us to do when the heat is turned up?
6. What were the results when Noah remained in the ark until God told him to come out?
7. Do you think Noah was tempted to jump out of the ark?
8. When Paul was shipwrecked, what temptation did the crew face?
9. What had to be cut from Paul's ship? Why?
10. What securities are you holding on to?
11. Why do you find it hard to let go of the things you hold on to?

chapter 9

Attitudes

One outstanding reason the Devil gets a hernia when we learn to say *no* is because he knows the awful, horrible attitudes that we will develop when we keep saying yes and take on more responsibilities than we can handle. Mary and Martha are prime examples.

Luke 10 paints a picture for us to carefully observe. Verse 38 says that as Jesus and his disciples were on their way, Jesus came to a village where a woman opened her home to him. Her name was Martha. According to *Strong's Concordance* (3136 Greek), Martha's name means "mistress." When I read what her name meant, I was hesitant to write about her. I always thought of a mistress as someone who is in an adulterous relationship with a married man. However, I believe her name fits the idea I am trying to bring across.

I believe that more and more people are falling out of love with Jesus, because they have taken on many lovers. Amongst their many lovers is one called *work*. Instead of being in love with Jesus and in love with their spouses, they are in love with and married to their work. That's what I call a spiritual adulterous love affair. Work can be our mistress as well if we are not careful. We spend most of our time, money, and energy on our work. It's that simple.

The word *mistress* has to do with women who are skilled in any kind of profession or skill. She knows how to control and rule and has authority over others or things and can be the head of an institution. I believe Martha wanted to rule and control this household, but because Mary was a woman who was able to sit at the feet of Jesus and listen to him, Martha or any one else would not and could not control her. I say, "Good for you Mary!" I believe Martha could have been very skilled and more than able to coordinate the women's ministry, the kitchen ministry, and the decorating committee, along with many other ministries. I believe she loved delegating the workload to others, but instead of delegating in love, she probably delegated in anger and got mad easily if women did not sign up to help her or do things her way. Her sister, Mary, was not into works, as Martha was. Mary could be found sitting at the Lord's feet, listening to what he said, whereas Martha was distracted by all the preparations that had to be made.

Mary was at Jesus' feet, listening, while Martha was *distracted* by all the preparations that had to be made. How many times have we been in prayer but not really listening to the voice of God? We were not listening because we were distracted by the voices screaming at us making demands of us, and trying to keep us busy. I can be in prayer and reading my Bible while my mind is working overtime with all the things I must *do* for the day. I hate when that happens, because it keeps me from hearing what God wants to say to me. Our minds cannot work overtime and listen to him all at the same time. We lose many battles with the Devil as he continues to throw distractions at us, but he has not won the war.

The Lord showed me something in Mark 5:25-33 about the woman with the issue of blood. This woman had to press through the crowd in order to touch the hem of the garment of Jesus to receive her healing. This woman needed a touch, and Jesus was not going to touch her until she pressed through. The Lord showed me that she not only pressed through the crowd, but also that with each person there was a voice. It is very hard to hear anything when others are talking. I cannot read and watch television at the same time.

The woman had to press through the many voices that could have distracted her from coming to Jesus and receiving all that he had for her.

She probably heard voices calling her unclean. Belittling voices asked her who she thought she was, coming to Jesus. She had to hear voices that kept reminding her how unworthy she really was. I am sure that there were voices that said it was impossible to touch the hem of his garment, because there were just too many people to press through. All kinds of people said all kinds of things that we cannot even imagine as she pressed through to touch the hem of his garment.

The bleeding woman is not the only one who has to press through. We all hear voices screaming at us, trying to not only dictate things to us, but also distract us from coming to Jesus. Those voices constantly scream at us. If we do not press through voices of condemnation that tear down our self-esteem or make us feel unworthy, there will be voices that keep reminding us of the many things we forgot to do yesterday, must do today, or deadlines that need to be met by tomorrow.

We also hear voices that tell us that what we do is not good enough. These voices tell us that we will never be good enough, so why not just give up? Inside each and every one of our minds is a recorder that keeps repeating our to-do list. "This is what needs to be done. This is what needs to be done. This was due yesterday. This is due now, and this is what is due tomorrow! This is what needs to be done. This is what needs to be done." Been there, done that, bought the jacket! Mary was at the feet of Jesus, however, not distracted but listening.

There is no way you can listen if you are distracted. You can also be at Jesus' feet but still be working. Your mind is putting in overtime, but you are not getting paid time and a half. Instead, your heart is divided in many directions. You are thinking about what to teach for Sunday school next Sunday or what to cook for dinner that night. *How am I going to get Susie to soccer practice on time?* We have distractions upon distractions.

Just the other day, I was sitting at my desk with an open Bible. I desired to pray and then read the Word. I read approximately one line of Scripture when I heard something. Oh no! Can you hear it? It is the sound of *silence!* It was the sound of a silent dryer. Just great! My clothes were dry. I had to take the clothes out of the dryer; I didn't want them to wrinkle. After I took them out of the dryer, I made up my mind that I would not fold them because I really wanted to pray and get in the Word. I threw them on the couch to fold later. *But wait! I better straighten them out so they won't wrinkle.* I laid them all out. (In the time it took me to do that, I could have folded them and had it done.)

On the way back to my study room, where I wanted to pray and read the Word, I realized that there were clothes in the washer that could be put in the dryer, because the dryer was empty. I did not want them to mildew and start stinking. Then I took the clothes out of the washer and put them in the dryer. After I put them in the dryer, I started to walk back to my study room. I was ready to pray and read the Word. But as I walked to my study room, my eyes took hold of the laundry hamper, and there was enough to start washing another load. I turned the washing machine on, and as it filled, I started to sort the clothes.

As I bent over to get more clothes to sort, I realized what the Devil was doing. He was distracting me with all the things that had to be done. Either I had to do the laundry, or else I would have to face dirty, mildewed, or wrinkled clothing.

Distraction brings confusion! It draws the mind in a totally different direction, and it can drive you insane if you do not get control over it. Remember Martha's name means *mistress,* which means a woman who rules others or has control, authority, or power over something or others. The Martha's of this world want to control the Mary's, but they are not even able to control or bring balance into their own lives.

I know this chapter deals with attitudes that take place when we take on more than God intended. Martha definitely developed an attitude toward her sister, Mary. She felt that she was left to do the work all by herself. When I hear people whining to me about all that they have to do, I want to say, "Who told you to do it? Did God tell you that you had to?" I know there are things in our lives that we must do. We have to go to work, do dishes, do laundry, etc.—but we can delegate. We don't have to do it all.

Even though I have no statistics to prove this particular statement, I have heard many say and many have agreed that about 10 percent of people do 90 percent of the work—not only in the church, but also in the home and in the workplace. Attitudes will begin to develop against people in the local church, the work place and at home. Before you know it, bitterness begins to takes root. That is exactly what Satan wants. He knows the power of unity. He knows that one can put a thousand to flight, and two can put ten thousand to flight. Psalm 133:1 says, "Behold how good and how pleasant it is for brethren to dwell together in unity."

Don't be ignorant of Satan's schemes or devices. He wants bitterness, conflicts, and a lack of unity among believers. I have seen people complain that no one helped them. However, whenever anyone offered to give them help, they refused the help. I do not like being around those kinds of people. I hate feeling guilty of not doing enough. People can make me feel that way, and I think that is one of the root problems of my busyness—guilt! *Guilt should never be a reason for doing anything!*

I believe that the 10 percent of the people who do all the work are equally as disobedient as the 90 percent of those who do not do a thing. If we all prayed and asked God what he wanted us to do, there would be more ministries in the church and less misery. Let us not forget that there will be fewer bad attitudes and more harmony in the body of Christ.

If 10 percent of the people do 90 percent of the work, they rob others of a blessing that God desires to give them. The blessing of being used of God and growing is very important. Those 10 percent who do 90 percent of the work have crippled others from walking out of their comfort zones. They enable inactive people to remain dormant in their pews and take on the stench of complacency. God made us human beings, not workhorses. We should only be concerned with being what he wants us to be and doing what he wants us to do. He expects us to take care of the temple.

Our bodies are the temple of the Holy Spirit. If we destroy our temples, he will destroy us. Many of our bodies are weak and sickly, because we overwork them. I read Ephesians 2, which said that we are God's workmanship and that he created us to do good works. It said *works*, not just *work*. In other words, it is okay to do more than one thing. However, if you can't chew gum and walk at the same time, like myself, you might take into consideration doing only one thing.

I looked up the word *good* in the Greek, and I noticed the word *well*. As God's workmanship, we need to take care of these bodies and our minds if we want to feel well and do well. I believe that he wants us to do good works, but he wants us to do them well. In other words, it is better to do one thing and do it well than take on more than one and not do so well.

A few years ago, I was taking the laundry down from the clothesline. Instead of taking a few pieces at a time and putting them in the basket, I tried to handle many towels, washcloths, sheets, and pillowcases. That would be great, but not all at the same time. God had me take a good look at this scene. (He has to teach me things in word pictures or illustrations for me to get his message!) As I took the clothes off the line, I was dropping them on the ground. All that laundry at one time was a little bit too much for me to handle.

As I kept gathering the clothes, I had to keep stopping to bend over to pick them up. It did not kill me to bend over and pick them up, but think of the time I could have saved and instead done something I really enjoyed. Because the girls' swimming pool was near the clotheslines, I dropped some of the clothes into the pool, and then I had to stop and wring them out. Unfortunately, after wringing all of the water out of the pool-drenched clothes, I had to hang them up all over again. This kept me from hanging up the next load of clothes, because I had to hang up the same clothes all over again. I began to learn that sometimes less is more. I remember watching *Angels in the Outfield* and hearing that statement. I never understood that until the day I dropped the laundry.

You are either a Martha who cannot listen or hear the voice of God because of the distractions due to all the things you have to do, or you are a Mary who can sit at the feet of Jesus and listen attentively to *all* he has to say. You are either a Martha who tries to control others to work as you do, or you are a Mary who has her priorities under the control of the Holy Spirit. You are either a Martha who has an attitude toward those who do not work like you, or you are a Mary who will submit to service in the Lord as the Holy Spirit leads her. There is a difference between working and serving. I always said I was laboring in love, when in reality I was laboring for God's love. Martha fit in the category of laboring for his love, and Mary served in love, as she did what she heard Jesus tell her in prayer.

If you are serving with a servant's heart for the Lord, you will have and maintain the love, joy, and peace that serving brings. Many of us fill positions of ministry and only display gripe fruit instead of the precious fruit of the Holy Spirit. Song of Solomon 1:2 says, "Let Him kiss me with the kisses of his mouth." This tells me to be kissed by the Son—to be Son-kissed!—and bear the fruit of the Holy Spirit, which is of love, joy, peace, kindness, gentleness, longsuffering, patience, self-control, and meekness. The Word says that we are branches, and we are to bear fruit. However, because of busyness, the fruit of the Holy Spirit is not developed from our branches. The only thing that develops is the weed of a bad attitude and gripe fruits. The choice is always ours to make.

I pictured Jesus giving me a kiss on the cheek and whispering, "Remember, it is okay to say no!"

Prayer: Father, I need to be like Mary, who can sit at your feet and listen attentively to what you have to say. I love being a Martha, but help me to maintain balance. Help me to delegate the things that need to be done if at all possible. Help me not to be critical when people don't do what I think they need to do. Give me a heart of gratitude, and take away all my bad attitudes. In Jesus name – Amen!

Time To Reflect

1. Do you consider yourself a Mary or a Martha? Explain your answer.
2. What distractions keep you from spending time with God?
3. Are you able to delegate authority, or do you feel you need to do the work yourself?
4. Are you in the category of believers who do 90 percent of the work, or are you in the category of believers who do only 10 percent of the work? Or do you do none of the work? Explain your answer.
5. Do you think God is pleased with the category you chose in the previous question? Explain your answer.
6. How is your attitude these days?
7. Are you Son-kissed each morning? Do you bear the fruit of the Holy Spirit, or do you produce sour gripe fruit because of all the distractions that come from your own busyness?
8. On a scale of one to ten, with ten being the highest and one being the lowest, where is your joy level?
   1__2__3__4__5__6__7__8__9__10__
9. We are God's workmanship, created to do good works and do them well. If you were told to rid yourself of any unfruitful activities, what activity or activities would God have you to prune away?

Prune faces are for those who refuse to prune away the activities that do not produce any fruit in their lives. Every morning, ask God to kiss you with the kisses of his mouth until you become Son-kissed and bear the precious fruit of the Holy Spirit.

chapter 10

Accusations

We have already discussed the story of Mary and Martha and how Martha was busy and distracted with all the preparations that she thought had to be made. However, Martha had a terrible attitude problem. Mary, on the other hand, sat at the feet of Jesus and listened attentively. Martha had attitude problems, because she felt it was all up to her to keep everybody happy, content, and satisfied. I sure have been there and done that. When you feel everyone's happiness depends on what you do, you are in a terrible place. You feel a heavy weight crushing you with the responsibility of keeping everyone happy and everything running smoothly.

Martha not only had an attitude problem, but also dealt with a problem of accusing. I believe we are most like the Devil when we accuse others or God. If you read Revelation 12:10, you will find that Satan is called the accuser of the brethren. If it is the nature of the Devil to accuse, then we are most like him when we do the same.

Martha accused Jesus of not caring. That is a lie from the pit of hell. Being uncaring is *not* his character or nature. His Word says that he wants us to cast all of our cares on him, because he cares for us. To think differently is to believe the lies of Satan. Psalm 139 tells us that he fearfully and wonderfully made us. He is acquainted with all of our ways. He tells us that he knows when we sit, lie down, and rise up. He knows the very words we think before we even speak them.

Jesus told us in Matthew 6:26-34 not to worry. He told us to consider the birds of the air and how he cares for them. When was the last time you watched the birds and saw them working hard? Never! Even our heavenly Father takes care of the birds of the air. Many of us toil, because we are not content with God's provisions. We begin to take on extra work to have a second income. We send mom off to work to pay for those extra credit cards. Then we wonder why we have the attitude problems that we have.

We are told to consider the lilies that neither toiled nor spun and how God clothed the fields as well. He told us that if we seek first his kingdom and righteousness, everything else would be added to us. Therefore, we know from his Word that God does care. He said sparrows are sold for a very small amount, but not one sparrow falls to the ground that he does not know about.

The birds of the air were sold; but we, as God's dear children, were bought with a price. The blood of Christ bought us at a great price, because he cares very much for us. He cares so much for us that he went to Calvary after suffering a terrible beating and scourging. How much does he love and care for you? Picture our Savior upon the cross with his arms opened wide. While we were yet sinners, he died for us because of his love and care for us. His arms are opened wide to receive us, but our hands are used to slap his face when we accuse him of not caring.

Martha accused Mary of leaving her with the workload. Who told Martha she had to do all the work? No one told Martha she had to take on all the responsibilities. How many times have we heard different people complaining about all they had to do? I want to ask, "Who told you that you had to do it?" If the Lord told someone to do something, I believe there would be joy and gladness in his or her heart. Psalms 100:2 specifically tells us that we need to serve God with gladness in our hearts. He also tells us in Colossians 3:17 that whatsoever we do in word or deed, do all in the name of the Lord Jesus, giving thanks to God and the Father by him.

It does not bring God glory if all we have are lousy, stinking attitudes. I don't care how much we do. Many of us say we are doing works for him, but if we really examine our hearts, we will find that we work for everyone but him. You not only do extra works for others, but also for yourself.

Our motive for doing anything should be because God asked us and because we love him enough to serve and obey him. God did not say that if we love him, we will do things for him and for others. He said in his Word that if we love him, we will obey him. You can do all the right things but do them for all the wrong reasons. We should be concerned about whether we are obeying God. We all need to ask ourselves, each time we make a commitment, "Why am I doing this activity?" Did God ask me to do it?" Many of us carry attitudes and accuse because we take on more than God expects us to take on. Is that you?

The Pharisees thought their prayers would be heard because they spoke often. Workaholics also seem to think that they will be seen and rewarded for all they do.

Time To Reflect

1. Do you accuse the Lord of not caring when you feel you are overloaded with work? If you do, then why?
2. Do you accuse others of leaving you with all the work?
3. What does your schedule look like these days?
4. Are you making commitments that drain you? If yes, explain why you make commitments that deplete your energy level.
5. Do you feel everyone's happiness depends on what you do? What are you going to do to change that?
6. Do you feel you have to keep everything running smoothly? If so, then what are you going to do to change that?
7. The Word tells us in Matthew 6:26-28 to behold the fowls of the air and the lilies of the field. It would take time for us to do

that. When was the last time that you took the time to consider God and his beautiful creation (in other words, take the time to smell the roses)? God saw his creation and said it was good.

8. Do you realize that you were bought with a price? Do you realize that you are fearfully and wonderfully made and that your body is the temple of the Holy Ghost?

9. God wants you to take time to care for yourself. What can you do to better care for yourself?

Prayer: I come to you with all my stinking attitudes. I have taken on too many responsibilities, accused you of not caring, and accused others of leaving me with the workload. Help me to delegate. Help me to serve you with gladness in my heart. In Jesus name – Amen!

chapter 11

Anger

This chapter has brought me much healing, because it exposed some root causes to a lot of pain in my life. As I read about the Prodigal Son's older brother, I felt emotional pain for this young man, because I have walked in his shoes a few times. Although it's tough for me to talk about, the Word tells us that love protects. I care about the salvation of others enough to keep my fingers still and not type the names of people who would know who I am referring to.

The prodigal son in Luke 15 spent all of his money after he left home. He did not spend it on righteous living but rather on riotous living. After his money was all gone, he had to do something quickly or starve. Finding a job was the next big thing he needed to add on his 'to-do' list. No one ever needs to pray about whether it is God's will to get a job if he or she has bills to pay. You should pray about where you should work and what kind of work God would have you do.

This prodigal's life hit bottom, and things needed to change. How many of us know that sometimes before our situations can change, *first we must change?* Many people think others need to change or circumstances need to change, but change starts with number one—*uno*—you! This is a profound truth. Some things will never change in life until we change. The Prodigal Son's change did not come until he found himself with no one to help him.

Most of the time, a place where you have no one there to help you can be the greatest place. I know that sounds crazy; however, I believe it to be true. Would you have to depend on God if someone was always there to rescue you from the messes that *you put yourself* in? No, I don't think so.

The prodigal son didn't find himself smelling like the pigs due to his good choices but because he had made some pretty bad choices. He reaped what he sowed. He not only smelled like the pigs, but also desired to eat what they ate. Have you ever been there? This is when he had a change of mind and a change of heart that led to a change of direction. It was then that he knew he had to wise up, rise up, return home, repent, and be reconciled with his father. This is true repentance. Would he have repented if someone were there to help him every time he found himself in a pickle? Others must have told him *no*—and rightly so.

Where was this prodigal's loving father all this time? His father was waiting patiently at home for him. Have you ever considered the fact that his father never went running after him? There was never any mention of the father getting upset and worried about how he spent the money. He did not get in his Mercedes and go looking for him. He was not too concerned about finding him to give him a lesson on how to spend his money wisely. The father also did not go looking for him to see if he needed another handout to make his life a bigger mess than it already was. The father had to let go and let God. He had to give up all control, let his son fall flat on his face, and let him rub his nose in the dirt—or should I say in the pig manure? Gross! I don't think anyone can go any lower than this. However, when the father chose to let go and let God, he got eternal results.

This is not just a story about the Prodigal Son and his father. It is not only a story about the Prodigal Son being restored to his father. There is another important person to consider—the Prodigal Son's older brother. I get a little irritated every time I read how the older brother was treated. The prodigal's brother, I feel, was not treated very fairly. The prodigal returned home, and the father put on a big feast for him and invited many—except for one family member, his older son.

God put this in Scripture for a very good reason. Many Christians carry the same attitude as this Prodigal Son's older brother and do not even know it. I believe God will allow situations to arise to show us our heart; however, God always sets choices before us. We can either choose to respond the way God intended us to when we feel we have not been treated fairly, or we can choose to be bitter and take matters into our own hands. The difference between bitter and better – is the 'I.' It is my choice how I respond.

The father loved this Prodigal Son so much that he treated him like royalty. The son was given clothes that were fit for the palace in exchange for his clothes that smelled like the pigpen. That was a great exchange, wouldn't you say? In the meantime, the older brother was out in the field, working up a sweat as a slave. His clothes probably stunk and were stained with sweat and soil. These clothes serve as a reminder of our self-righteousness, which is as filthy rags when we try to obtain favor from the Father by our works.

While the older brother was working, he heard a sound. It was the sound of music. The father threw a celebration for his squandering son, and no one invited the older son to the feast. What kind of deal was this? If I looked at this situation without knowing the Scriptures about unfair treatment, I would say it was a raw deal. The older brother had to humble himself and ask someone, "Why the music?"

Is it any wonder the older brother had an attitude? How would you feel? I don't know about you, but I know I would have been ticked, hurt, rejected, insulted, and felt no one cared. His brother was missing in action, and not one person had the decency to tell him that his brother was very much alive or give him an invitation. Jesus is alive as well, and what are we doing to tell others that he is alive? Do we give people an invitation to salvation? I can get upset with those who did not tell this older brother that his little brother was alive, but am I telling others that Jesus is alive and that in an hour we do not expect, *he is returning* as well?

The older brother was so angry that he refused to go in and celebrate once he found out his brother was home. Sometimes that is wise. It may have been better not to go in if he had an attitude. His father went out and pleaded with him to come inside. I can comprehend his hurt and anger. He said, "Look! All these years, I have been slaving for you and never disobeyed your orders! Yet you never gave me even a young goat so I could celebrate with my friends. But when this son of yours—who has squandered your property with prostitutes, booze, and drugs—comes home, you go and kill the fatted calf for him." The brother never recognized his sibling. He said, "This son of yours."

Here comes the stinker! Listen and smell the stench of self-righteousness that came out of the older brother's mouth: "I have been slaving. I never disobeyed orders"—as if his dad was a drill sergeant. We must remember that the Prodigal Son had the smell of the pigs all over him due to his choice to live riotously. I believe that as bad as pigs smell, an even stronger and more repulsive stench filled the atmosphere at this point. It was the stench of a self-righteous attitude and bitterness, which always lead to anger. The Word says that our righteousness is as filthy rags. Yes, he was angry, but the root of that anger was self-righteousness and thinking he deserved to be treated much better.

If we all got what we deserved, we would not be here to tell about it. The older son said he never disobeyed. Yeah, right! He told his father he had been slaving for years. If you do not have a servant's heart, you will think the same thoughts about others who are blessed by the Father, especially if they don't deserve his grace. That is what grace and mercy are all about. There is another way to look at the older son. He may not have had a self-righteous attitude but simply been hurt.

I can recall a time when I told God I hated someone. I hit the floor and told God, "I hate this person! I hate this person!" (Yeah, it was a temper tantrum!) God let me know that I did not hate but that I was hurt—and there is a difference. Let God show you your heart. Let him tell you if you feel hate, hurt, or jealousy. I hope you don't object to another true story.

When I lived in Brownsville, New York, I felt depressed one day and took a long nap. When I woke up, I knew that something was not right in me. I could not put my finger on it but asked God to show me what the problem was. I asked God why I felt so depressed and angry. It was a silent anger. Before I left the bed, I felt like I'd seen handwriting on the wall. I envisioned one word—*resentment*.

I remember asking the Lord why he did not say the word *hate* or *angry*. When I looked up the word in the dictionary, I came to understand why I saw the word *resentment*. *Resentment* was defined as feelings of anger caused by slight or being made to not feel very important. I had gone through much rejection in life, and I was still in need of healing. Many people made me feel worthless and useless. I was made to feel that I had nothing to offer anyone, and I carried a silent bomb of silent anger inside myself. I was not invited to many events in life. Anything I suggested was ignored, and I felt intimidated whenever God wanted to use me. I always listened to Satan's lies that whispered loudly, "Who do you think you are?" However, I have come a long way!

I never thought I had the older brother's attitude until recently. One day, a good friend of mine told me that he had received a $200 bonus. It was not Christmas. Was it his birthday? No. What was the occasion? There was none. It was a free gift. God used another person to bless my friend. I saw the older brother's attitude rise up in me quickly, and it smelled pretty rotten. "What gives, God?"

The night before, the Lord told me to give $100 to a particular ministry. God showed me my self-righteous attitude. I was hesitant about giving, but I knew God was prompting me to give. Did I reap a blessing? Not that I could see. No, instead the very next day, I got a call stating that God had blessed my friend with not $100, but $200! *What? How can that be? Lord, I gave $100 last night. I go to church every time the doors are opened up, not him!*

Words of self-righteousness gushed out of me like a tsunami. I needed a blood bath—in the blood of Christ. I stunk! Then I realized, *Hey this is God's grace. Grace is not earned or worked for. It is not anything I have done, am doing, or ever will do.* Guess what, folks; it is not about *me!* It is not because of who I am or anything that I have done but because of *who he is and what he already did at Calvary!*

Grace is God's precious, unmerited favor, given from him to us with love. It cannot get any better than that. When we realize that we are saved by grace through faith in Christ Jesus, we will rejoice when others receive God's blessings by grace. We can never earn our salvation. We can never earn healing or deliverance. We can never work for it or buy it. We will never deserve it. It is a free gift. All we have to do is receive it freely. If we all got what we deserved, I would not be writing this, and you would not be reading. Thank God we do not get what we deserve. We would all be doomed.

Our righteousness is as filthy rags. Who wore the clothes that smelled like the pigs? It was the prodigal son. However, when he rose up and went to his father with a repentant heart, his father embraced him and gave him a robe and a ring and rejoiced. The angels rejoice when one sinner comes to repentance. We need to get rid of our rotten, stinkin' thinkin' and begin to rejoice when the prodigal comes home, because it is only by the grace of God there goes I!

To the church of the Lord Jesus Christ:

We need to share with the lost the fact that Jesus is alive and that he, too, is returning on a day or hour that no one knows.

Time To Reflect

1. How did you feel when a prodigal came back home or to church and got all the attention?
2. If you were a prodigal at one time, how were you treated when you came back home? Did you get what you deserved?
3. Why is it a good thing when there is no one to help rescue you from your messes that you put yourself in?
4. What was the result of no one helping the Prodigal Son?
5. Where was the father while the prodigal was MIA?
6. Should we always go after the prodigals? Why or why not?
7. Do you think the father's treatment of both his Prodigal Son and his older son was fair?

8. What stunk worse—the stench of pigs or the older brother's attitude? Have you ever stunk from self-righteousness? Explain.

9. What was the older brother's attitude toward his father and brother?

10. Would you have entered the prodigal's party if you were not invited? Why or why not?

11. Do you feel the older brother had a self-righteous attitude, or was he just hurt? How would you feel if you were in his place?

12. Did the older brother have a right to be angry? Why or why not?

Jesus, like the Prodigal Son, was dead and is now alive. Just as the Prodigal Son *returned* after *rising*, Jesus has *risen* and is *returning!* Have you given an invitation to those who do not know him?

Prayer: Father, I come to you with all of my anger, self-righteousness, and hurt. Help me to rejoice when others are blessed. Help me to be obedient and do what you want me to do regardless of whether I see the blessing here on earth. Help me to rejoice and not be jealous when the prodigals come back to the Father's house. In Jesus name - Amen!

chapter 12

God's Answer To Overcoming Busyness

We are finally in the last section of the book. We have discussed reasons we choose to stay busy and reasons the Devil wants to keep us busy. He wants us busy so he can bind us and bring about burnout. Sometimes people think we are running strong because we haven't quit. The Devil may not be able to get us to quit, but if he can keep us bound to busyness and cause us to be burnt out, he has succeeded. He knows that if we are bound, we will not be able to function under the Holy Spirit's unction, and if we are burnt out, we cannot shine in a dark place.

Several years ago, God shared a truth that totally set me free. God took me to Genesis 1, and I began to see more insights than just the creation story. I realized that he created me with a purpose, and if I was to be effective, I had to listen and do only what he said. In other words, I had to do things his way.

On the first day of January, I read Genesis 1—"in the beginning!" *"What more can one learn about the creation story?"* I thought. I had the same attitude as one having leftover meatloaf for the third night. We all know God spoke, and it was so. God let me know that before anything was created, he had to *speak*. After he *spoke*, he *set* things where he wanted them. After he *set* everything where he wanted it, everything *served* its purpose as God created it.

God told me that if he has not told me to do certain works or ministries, then I am setting myself up in those positions or ministries as well as setting myself up for heartache, disappointment, and most of all, burnout. When God has not spoken and is not setting me where it pleases him, I cannot serve effectively, as God purposed. His Word declares in I Corinthians 12:18 that God places every member where it please and not where he or she pleases.

God had and still has my attention in this area. I am only to do what he wants me to do. I should only want to go where he wants me to go, and I should only want to say what he wants me to say. I should want nothing more or nothing less. I don't want to be like Rachel, who named her child Joseph, because I want God to give me another ministry, position, occupation, or child because of my desperate need to be constantly assured of his (and others) love and acceptance. He loves me. He loves you. We all need to receive that love.

I believe if we handle more than two (and maybe even more than one) ministries, God may tell us to renounce, relinquish, or release some things. If we can't, then we need to search our hearts and ask why. Do we refuse because of selfish ambition; pride; ego; a need for approval, acceptance, or attention; or a way of earning our way to heaven? I cannot and will not tell you what you should release. However we all need to search our hearts and ask God what he would have us release to please him. Release to please!

God has taught me several practical lessons to show me that I need to let go. In the first lesson, he used my debit card. Not only did he let me know that I hold on tightly, but he also gave me a small glimpse of how he feels when we can't let go. I know I grieve the Holy Spirit when I hang on tight and refuse to let go of fear, attitudes, or things when he asks me to.

I was looking for my debit card. I thought it was in my pocket, but when I went to get it, the card had vanished. Then I remembered that it was in my pants pocket after all. Even though it started out in my pants pocket, I did not find it there. I washed the pants. Luckily, I took the clothes out of the washer, and it was at the bottom of the washing machine. I was not sure if I would even be able to use it again.

After I pulled the card out of the washer, I placed it on top of the washer. My granddaughter, Chelsey, decided to have some fun with me. After finding my card, she came to me and asked, "What hand, Grandma?" I was not in any mood to play games. I had much to *do* that day, and I just wanted her to release the debit card to me. I remember getting a little perturbed with her! I was upset with her, because she would not release the card to me. I could see I was getting nowhere, so I said, "Forget it!" It was no longer a game. This is when I saw how God must feel when I hold on for dear life to things; such as anger, attitudes, bitterness and etc. and refuse to release them to him. He wants me to surrender my all to him. I also saw how fast Chelsey released the card to me when I said, "Forget it."

That was a lesson on surrender. I have seen over and over again that when God says to release something, he means I should release it. There is something in all of us that likes to feel like we are in control. The truth is that we are not in control. Whatever we hold on to and can't let go of definitely has control of us. What will it take for us to surrender our all? I am very thankful that God is patient! When we let go, he gives back much more, and he gives us what is best for us.

I work with preschool children. One day, I observed two children playing with a toy. The two children wanted the same toy. I watched them both hang on for dear life. No one wanted to let go. God showed me myself in that scene, and it was not a pretty picture. God showed me that in order for me to release some things in my life he just about has to pry my fingers off one finger at a time. People laugh when I demonstrate to them how God pries my fingers off—one finger at a time. But honestly, it is not a laughing matter.

God also began to share with me the great wisdom of Solomon (1 Kings 3:16–28). The two prostitutes in this story had much in common. They both had sons, and they not only lived in the same house, but also shared the same bed. Both of these women had everything in common—or did they? Apparently, one of these ladies rolled over on her son, and he died.

There was one big problem, however. Neither of them was willing to let go of the living baby.

These ladies tried to claim the same living baby. Both were brought before Solomon with their case. Solomon had to put the cutting edge to the problem. Talk about advice! He said, "Bring out the sword, and let's cut the baby in half." There was a moment of truth. This is where we find that the women didn't share the same interest. One mother was in total agreement. *Ouch!* She was not very motherly, was she? Fortunately for the baby, the true mother was willing to give him up or let go of the very thing she loved the most in order to keep her child alive.

God asked me, "Are you willing to let go and let God? Are you willing to let go of the very things you love in order to keep the thing you love alive?" God had already shouted at me to get out of the way! I wish I could tell you I got out of the way right away, but I didn't. I was not willing to let go. What would people think? Would they think I was kicked out of the ministry? Would someone come along and do better than me? That hurts and strips away at your pride. Would people not need me anymore? Would people think less of me?

I don't think I was worried about God and how he would feel. I was worried about number *one—me!* Solomon asked for a sword to cut the baby in half. Maybe God is saying to us today, "Bring out the sword that is sharper than any two-edged sword that is a discerner of the thoughts and knows the intents of the heart, and cut in half some activities in your life that may not produce any fruit." What are your intentions? Why do you do the things you do? Bring out the sword! Bring out the sword of the Spirit, which is the Word of God. Let it show *your* intentions, and then let it cut the workload in half. It will not only cut the workload in half, but also cut away the wrong motives and intents of the heart.

Titus 2 tells us that God's grace teaches us to say no. If you read that chapter in its entirety, it tells us what we are to say no to. We are to say no not only to ungodliness, but also to worldly passions. We are also to live self-controlled, upright, and godly lives. *You mean I have to have self-control?*

Self-control can cover a lot of territory. I have always seen that I need self-control over my eating, emotions, spending, how much time I spend watching television and talking on the telephone. Now I see that we all need self-control when it comes to how much work or how many ministries we take on. Many of us are out of control in this area. We can do all the right things but for all the wrong reasons, as we have discussed in previous chapters.

Not being able to say *no* is the wrong reason to be involved in a ministry. Being in a ministry because your pastor or pastor's wife asked you is the wrong reason. Being in a ministry because you are gifted can be a wrong reason as well. The question you need to ask yourself is this: "Did God call me?" I know there will be many who disagree with me. God is not calling me to be popular, but he is calling me to be obedient. I am not saying that you can't use your gifts and talents. God expects us to use them. *Use it or lose it,* I say. But there must be balance, and we must use our gifts and talents where God places us.

Remember the question, "Why do you do the things you do?" Are you doing things for assurance of your salvation? Do you feel others won't accept you if you say no? Do you assume that because an activity is spiritual, God will bless your efforts? Are you afraid to tell others no when they ask you to do something? What emotional pain are you trying to avoid?

Have you checked your attitude these days? Do you get angry that others have left you to do all the work? Do you accuse God of putting too much on you, or do you think others expect too much of you? Do you accuse God of not caring? Do you feel like you have been slaving for years, and God and others have showed you no appreciation? These are a few reasons you may choose to stay busy. The Devil wants to keep you busy. He wants you bound to bad attitudes, anger, and accusations. The Devil will work overtime trying to keep you working overtime.

I pray that God has revealed some root causes for your busyness. God wants us to enjoy life to the fullest. God wants us to have peace and joy— even in the toughest of circumstances. We will be able to enjoy the journey God has for us if we are obedient to him and do only the things he asks us to do. If we do only the things he asks of us, we will be able to find time to spend with him and with our loved ones and friends.

God created us to be in relationships. First, he wants us to be in a right relationship with him. When we are in a relationship with him, we will hear his voice, and then we should do only what he says to do. Second, he wants us to be in good relationships with others. He created us for fellowship and relationships. Take the time now, and start prioritizing. Ask God to show you what he requires of you and what to prune away that produces no fruit. Remember, only as God speaks will he set you where it pleases him in his time. As we do, then everything will serve its purpose as God has planned for your life.

The Lord had to remind me that I was out of balance *once again!* I was working with preschool children. The master teacher, Ms. Sarah, was taking attendance. When she called each child by name, the child was to respond and say, "Here!" As she was halfway through the attendance, I heard her tell the children not to say anything unless she called their names. Everyone said "here," even when his or her name was not called.

When she said those words, something quickened in my spirit. I knew that God was speaking through her to me. The next morning, I started journaling the experience. God took me to Isaiah 6, where Isaiah also said, "Here am I; send me." However, the Lord had me read the previous verses. Isaiah was able to say, "Here am I," because he heard the voice of the Lord. Then the Lord asked Isaiah himself whom he could send. Isaiah was able to say, "Here am I." After he heard the voice of the Lord asking whom he should send, he responded, and the Lord gave him divine direction.

The Lord began to share with me that many of us are not effective, because we say, "Here am I" when God is not calling us—just as the children in the class said, "Here" when Ms. Sarah was not calling them. If God is not calling us, he is also not giving us divine direction on how to do something. We should not do whatever it is we are doing.

A lady I know wants to begin a ministry in her church. I thought it was great, but then she told me she was going to her pastor after another sister wrote down all the things she did when she was at her church and gave it to this sister so she could start this ministry. I told my sister in the Lord that she should not get her ideas from what this other sister *used* to do. If God had called her to this ministry, God would give her the blueprint on how to do it—just as *he* gave divine directions to Isaiah. First, God calls us. Then—and not until then—respond and say, "Here am I," and then let him give the divine blueprint. Otherwise, your effort will not be for God, but for yourself!

The best part of this story is that I began to write everything I did in the church. When I wrote the word *youth,* I put a question mark next to it. I was helping with the youth group for a couple of weeks but I really did not feel God wanted me there. I was afraid to tell the youth leader that I felt God wanted me to stay downstairs with the adults and my husband; however, I did not have to say a word. God confirmed that he did not want me working with youth, because when I went to the youth leader, he told me that another woman came forward to help. I love it when God confirms like that.

Let's eavesdrop on a conversation between Jethro and Moses. Jethro was the father-in-law of Moses, and he gave some pretty good advice that we should also heed. In Exodus 18, Jethro told Moses that what he was doing was not good. However, Moses was doing a good thing. Moses had judged the people, but they kept Moses busy from morning until evening. Jethro asked him a very sensible question. He wanted to know why Moses was doing all the judging by himself.

Moses told Jethro that the people came to him to inquire of God for them. Jethro told Moses that what he was doing was not good and that if he continued to not delegate, he would definitely burn out. Moses needed a plan, and Jethro was just the guy who could help. Jethro suggested that Moses teach the people the decrees and laws, show them how to live, and teach the duties that they were to perform. Jethro told Moses that if he would do this, his load would be made lighter. That sounds like a plan—and team work. People would have a part in sharing the workload with Moses.

In Exodus 18:23, Jethro said that if Moses followed his advice and God so commanded, Moses would be able to stand the strain, and the people would be able to go home satisfied. What did Moses have to lose? What do we have to lose? How many times have we been like Martha and felt like there was no one there to help us? How many times have we felt that someone has left us with all the work, including Jesus? How many have worked from morning until evening because people kept coming with a long list of things for us to do?

In the beginning, God gave Adam a helper, because God knew that Adam could not go through life alone. Moses couldn't, and neither can we. God has *one body*, but he provided many members to delegate the workload to. Sometimes we can have the same attitude as the eye had toward the hand in 1 Corinthians 12; we feel we don't have need of others. If you feel that way, then you are deceived. We need others to help us.

We need to start training younger ones and teach others how to ask things of God for his or her self instead of feeling we have to ask God for them. We need to do what Jethro told Moses to do. Teach others about God's Word and his ways. Show them how God wants them to live and the duties they are to perform! Listen to God. What does he want you to do? Just do it! What does he want others to do? David knew what God required of him and what he required of Judah and his son, Solomon. You do not have to please others, as Aaron did, and lead people in idolatry. You do not even have to prove anything to yourself.

I truly believe that when you please God, you will please others and yourself. You will be content, and so will others. I believe God looks down and smiles at those who know who they are and where they belong in the body of Christ. Everyone is important and necessary in the body of Christ. We don't have to compare and compete, as Rachel and Leah did, to obtain favor with God or others. Never assume, like David and Nathan, that it's okay to build a temple—even though it's for the Lord—because it may *not* be okay. Are you still hiding between a wall and a refrigerator out of fear someone might ask you to do something? Get guts! Say *no!* Don't think you have to always do something to obtain or earn salvation, as the jail keeper and the rich young ruler thought. You can quit burying your emotional pain in the dirt of works.

It does not matter whether you are a foot, hand, eye, ear, mouthpiece, the heart, or liver. *All* members are necessary. Did you hear that? You are *necissito!* You have such a nature that you must exist. Even though you *must* exist, God wants more for your life. He does not want you to feel like you only exist. God wants *you* to have a life that you can enjoy to the fullest. More important than anything else, he wants you to have life, because he wants others to obtain eternal life. How can you reach them if you are bound, busy, or burnt out?

Let your little light shine, and don't let Satan blow it out! Wait a minute! Many times, the Devil gets blamed for things he did not even do. Satan cannot blow your light out any more than anyone can separate you from the love of God, which is in Christ Jesus. The only one who can separate you from the love of God is *you!* The only one who can put your lights out is *you!* The only one who can cause you to lose your passion is *you!* You have to guard your heart.

Until you find out why you go beyond the call of duty when God is not requiring you to do whatever you are doing, you will be busy, bound, and burnt out. You will not be effective until you allow the two-edged sword to cut away the roots and every wrong motive for doing the things you do. It may seem that a candle burning at both ends will shine even brighter. You may, but it won't be long before the candle will be used up and good for nothing.

As you do only the things God wants you to do, you will be free to enjoy life to the fullest and shine brightly in a dark and lost world. There are people God wants all of us to reach, but we need the light to find them in the dark. God has given us that light—but use it the way he intended.

www.ingramcontent.com/pod-product-compliance
Lightning Source LLC
Chambersburg PA
CBHW030358290526
45785CB00004B/1814